DITCH

YOUR THINKING

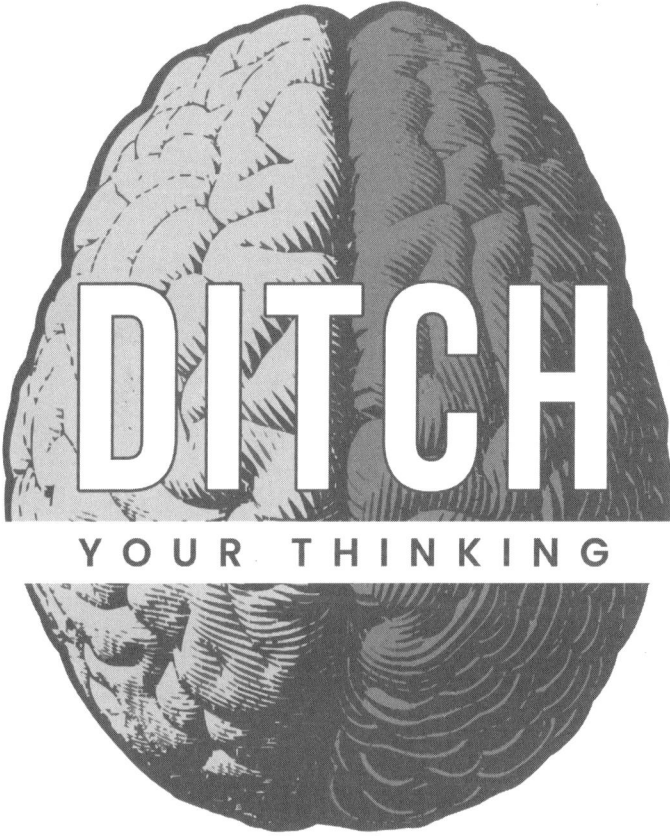

FREEDOM FROM ANXIETY, FEAR, WORRY, AND MORE

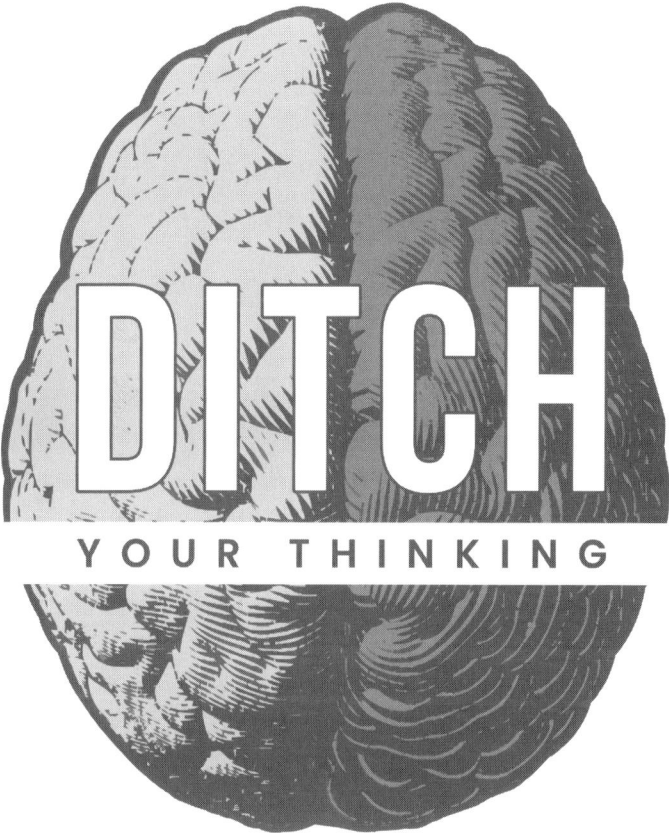

DITCH

YOUR THINKING

FREEDOM FROM ANXIETY, FEAR, WORRY, AND MORE

SCOT LONGYEAR

Cover design by Michael Bates
Interior design by Russell Lake

Library of Congress Control Number: 2020942430

ISBN 978-1-7325990-1-7

PRINTED IN THE UNITED STATES OF AMERICA

Dedicated to those who
desperately want to
be to be free.

Special thanks to my partner and best friend Stephanie. You put up with much! I am grateful to my daughters - Mariah and Madison - and their husbands (my sons) Isaac and Jacob.

I am grateful to my extended family, friends, and community of Christ followers who continually encourage me to put words to page.

Thanks to the team who linked arms with me on this project: Al and Tracie Denson, Anna Lowe, Ellen Tucker Krumreich, Brandi Koie, Russell Lake, Michael Bates, Brian Dorsett, David Williamson, and many more. If a man's wealth is determined by his family and friends, I am filthy rich.

Contents

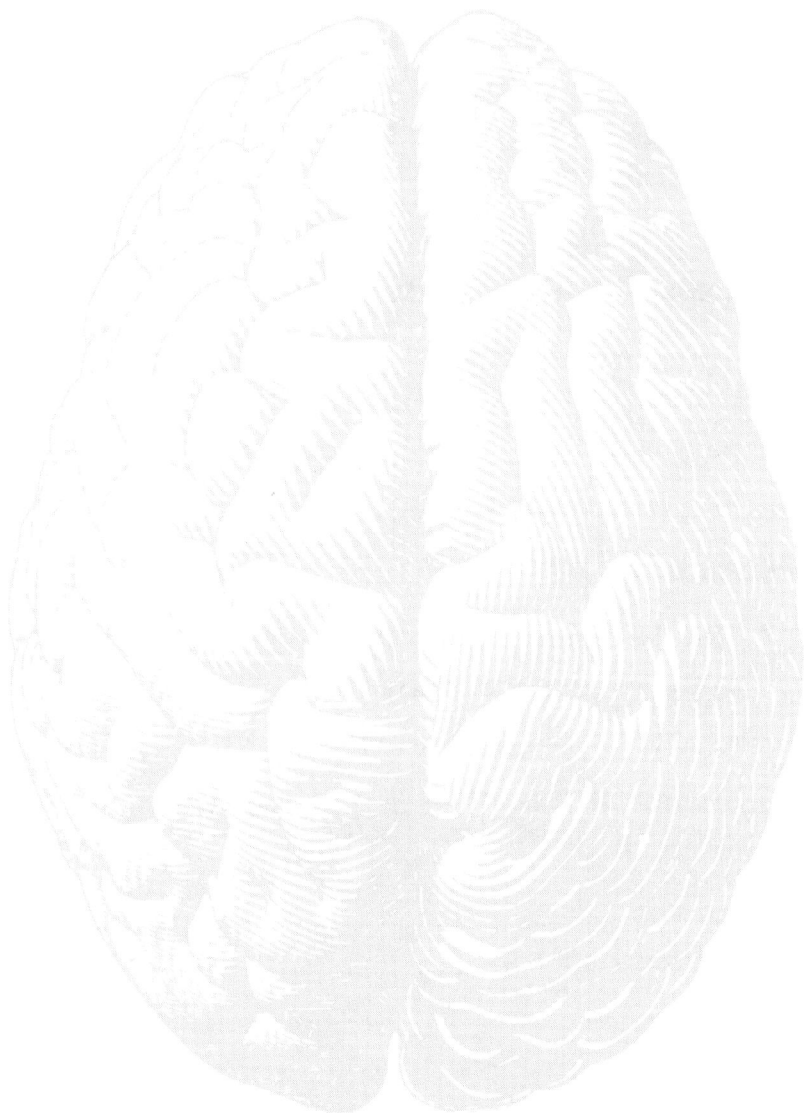

Introduction

To other people, it looks like we have it all together. If they only knew that just underneath the surface we struggle with doubt, fear, anxiety, and more. We worry all the time. When we are not worrying, we are worried that we are forgetting something to worry about. We wonder if peace is even a remote possibility.

It is.

What if you could sleep tonight with no worries?

What if you could wake up in the morning with zero anxiety?

What if, tomorrow, you left fear behind?

Friend, it *is* possible.

I wrote this book for all of us. We are strugglers. We are stuck. We believe in a better way, but we have yet to find it. The fight is real. There is a way out. This book you are holding will help navigate your journey to freedom. In the following pages, you will learn the *DITCH Method.* I personally designed and use this system in order to gain freedom from negative thoughts. As we take control of our thoughts, our entire lives change. How we think directly affects the quality of our lives. That's why the Apostle Paul challenges us to ". . . be transformed by the renewing of your mind" (Romans 12:2).

In other words, if we change our thinking, we can change our lives. It may sound far-fetched, but science is proving this to be true. In a documented scientific study, researchers concluded that "12 minutes of daily focused prayer over an 8 week period can change the brain to such an extent that it can be measured on a brain scan."[1] Science is proving what the Bible says: We are changed by our thinking.

> **If we change our thinking, we can change our lives.**

In this book you will learn how to apply the *DITCH Method* to every negative thought. As you run this simple framework, you will find hope, freedom, and peace. In addition, we will dive into scripture and learn how God wants to use our emotions for good. For example, did you know that He wants to use your sadness to fuel your influence? Or your disappointment to bring hope? He has a purpose for you, and He works everything together for the good of His kids – including using our negative emotions to bring about life change (Romans 8:28).

I want to make sure that I am not misunderstood. This is not a "me-centered" practice. This is a framework where we submit to the work of the Holy Spirit, follow Jesus with all that we have, and direct our thoughts to do the same. This actually has little to do with us and everything to do with Christ.

Imagine a new life of freedom, a life where the Holy Spirit controls your thoughts instead of your thoughts controlling you. If you are ready for a change, the time is now. *DITCH* your thinking and find the life you have always dreamed of.

> "We demolish arguments and every pretension that sets itself up against the knowledge of God, and we take captive every thought to *make it obedient to Christ*" (2 Cor 10:5; emphasis mine).

Prelude

When I was a kid, my friends and I would play "Ditch." The rules were simple. Someone would yell "Ditch!" followed by a name. Often one of my pals would yell, "Ditch Scot!" Everyone else would run away as fast as they could, all in different directions. It was my job to run after them and try to tag them. Nothing was out of bounds. They could run, hide, climb a tree, or bury themselves in a hole. When my name was called, my friends scattered; I was left alone. I was "ditched."

It's high time we ditch our thinking. Let's call out our negative emotions ("*DITCH* fear! *DITCH* anger! *DITCH* guilt!") and start running.

Here we go!

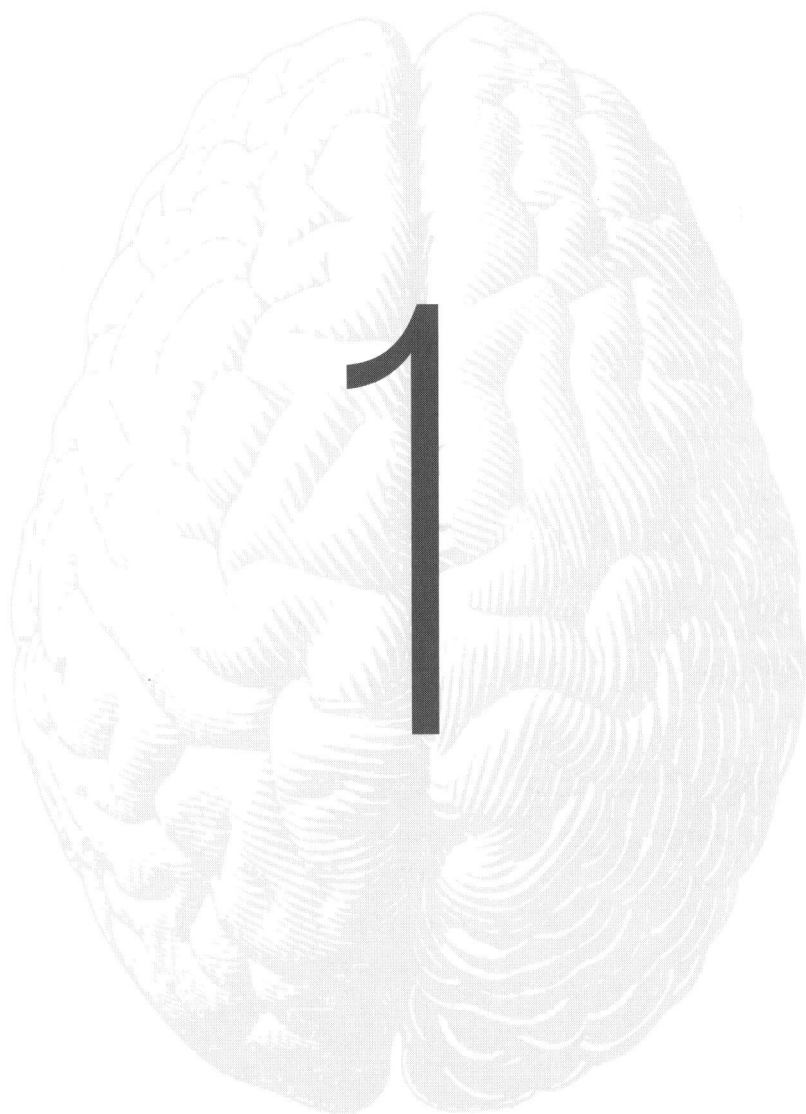

1

DITCH

It was 10:30 on a Saturday night. I was in bed. I wouldn't say I cried myself to sleep, but it was close. My eyes welled up with tears. My mind was racing. My body was housing anxiety, fear, and maybe some anger. I wanted to simultaneously yell and cry. Feeling completely defeated, I let out a huge sigh.

"What is wrong with me?"

Nothing. And everything.

If you took stock of my life, you would conclude that I should not feel this way. I have a great family. I married way out of my league. My kids are smart (they received their intelligence from Mom) and beautiful (again, Mom). I live in a nice house. I don't want for my next meal. Our church is one of the fastest growing in the nation. We have a healthy staff. We see people take massive steps closer to Christ every week. I have deep friendships. I have good physical health. I am able to travel. I am ridiculously blessed. My life looks like I have it all together. And I do. But I don't. How could a life so *right* feel so *wrong?*

In bed, my mind melted over the thought of preaching the next day. In less than 12 hours I would stand on a platform and speak to a large number of people both live and on video. The thought of the platform started to erode my mind. But here is the crazy thing: I had nothing to fear. I have preached hundreds of times.

> How could a life so *right* feel so *wrong?*

I knew the content of the sermon was solid. No one would heckle me (at least I hoped). When I wrote the sermon, I prayed, and God led me to great passages and stories. Preaching is my thing. It's what I am made to do. Yet there I was, nearly crying myself to sleep. While nothing seemed wrong, something was not right.

That's when I again realized what I know to be true - this whole game of stress, anxiety, anger, and pressure - it's not external, it's internal. It's a mind game. That's why the Apostle Paul says:

"Do not conform to the pattern of this world, but be transformed by the renewing of your mind . . ." (Romans 12:2).

Friend, the battle is not won by changing our circumstances. It is won by *changing our minds.* When we change the way we *think* about our circumstances, everything changes. Paul says it clearly: If you want to transform your life, change your thinking.

Maybe you have some anxiety, worries, fear, frus-tration, or you're feeling 20 other emotions all at once. What if you could be free from all that garbage? What if you could live in peace, even if your circumstances are chaotic?

> If you want to transform your life, change your thinking.

What if you could have no worries, even while your home life and job life are not perfect? According to Romans 12, it is possible. The solution? Renew our mind. Get out of the rut and start living in the way that God designed us to live.

The DITCH method is a scripture-based framework which helps us renew our minds (remember, a new mind results in transforming our lives.) I use this method to get my thinking back on track. When a worry comes into my mind, I run it through the DITCH method. This tool helps beat down the lies, form new thoughts in the mind, and allows us to live with the freedom we have been searching for.

In this chapter I will lay out the DITCH method. This serves as our foundational tool. The method will help us identify one of eight primary negative emotions. In the chapters following, we will explore how we apply the DITCH method to each of these emotions.

So, let's say your mind is spinning, and you know something is off. Once you run those thoughts through the DITCH method, you identify that the primary emotion is anxiety. Flip to chapter 6 where we explore what it is like to transform out of anxiety by renewing our minds.

In the following chapters, we will also look at how God can *redeem* some potential negative emotions. For example, did you know that sometimes God actually wants us to be angry? But I am getting ahead of myself. More on that in the next chapter.

So, how do we DITCH the negative thoughts? Glad you asked!

DETERMINE THE EMOTION

The shortest verse in all of scripture is John 11:35. John simply reports that "Jesus wept." Obviously, there is a bigger story at play here, but John shows an *emotion* that came to the surface; our Jesus had tears in His eyes. But tears are not the emotion. Crying is not an emotion. To get to the emotion, we must get beyond what the emotion presents (in this case, the emotion is presenting tears).

To determine the emotion, we look at the *external* action (crying, yelling, stuffing our face in a pint of ice cream, sleeping all day) and ask ourselves, "What *emotion* is causing this action?" Our actions will likely be tied to one of the following emotions:

- Anger
- Annoyance (a weaker form of anger)
- Sadness
- Guilt
- Anxiety / Fear
- Discouragement
- Apathy
- Disappointment

In the case of Jesus crying, the emotion was

likely a mixture of sadness (because His friend had died) and disappointment (because some of His followers were blaming Him for the death - John 11:21).

When determining an emotion, it is important to remember that the presented issue is not always the actual issue. For example, years ago a friend and I were at odds. We had done some work together, and let's just say that it didn't go well. We finally decided to sit down and talk it out. My friend was angry. He made a long list of the actions that I had done wrong. He was obviously upset. I was a bit confused because I didn't think that my actions matched his level of anger. Once he stopped talking, I just looked at him and said (not in anger), "What is this *really* about?" He paused, dropped his head, and said, "Scot, I really don't know."

> **The presented issue is not always the actual issue.**

In the case above, the presenting emotion was not the *real* emotion. My friend was presenting anger, but, when we dug around, we found that it was really an emotion of discouragement.

Again, to find the emotion, we ask ourselves, "What *emotion* is causing this action?"

When determining the emotion, make sure to spend some time to draw a straight line from the external action to the correct emotion. Once we have determined the correct emotion, we are ready to move to the next step.

IDENTIFY THE STRONGHOLD

The Bible makes several references to strongholds. Some of those references are positive. For example, Psalm 18:2 references a stronghold as a fortress or place where we are protected.

However, the Bible often talks about strongholds in the negative sense and suggests that we need to tear down strongholds.

"For though we live in the world, we do not wage war as the world does. The weapons we fight with are not the weapons of the world. On the contrary, they have divine power to demolish strongholds" (2 Corinthians 10:3-4; emphasis mine).

What is a stronghold? In ancient times the term "stronghold" was used to describe a prison or a fort made of rock. It was also used figuratively as a "false argument in which a person seeks shelter."[2] Very simply, a stronghold is a lie that keeps us trapped.

My friends, the Yegerlehners, are dairy farmers. Each year, they recruit a large group of friends for what they call the "Cattle Drive." The job? Move 75 head of cattle from one field to another. When first asked to be part of this, I imagined we would throw on a large hat, grab some nice cowboy boots, saddle up, gallop back and forth across a field and yell "yee-ha." After all, I had seen cattle drives in the movies, so I was kind of an expert. When I arrived on "Cattle Drive Day," I found out that I was wrong. Very wrong. There was a better method to moving 75 cattle from one field to another: We would present a stronghold (a lie) to the cattle.

The fields were about 1/4 mile from each other. To get the cows from one field to the next would require them walking down a local county road. Evidently, cows do not understand directions and don't have the opposable thumbs necessary to use Waze, but they still needed to travel the road. So, we would escort them down the road. Laughable, right? How in the world can a person

> **Very simply, a stronghold is a lie that keeps us trapped.**

control a 1000-pound cow? Again, all we had to do was use a stronghold (lie).

> How in the world can a person control a 1000-pound cow?

The crowd of friends (about 100 of us) lined up on each side of the road where the cows would travel. Strung out on each side of the road was a ridiculously long (like 1/4 mile) and ridiculously thin piece of string. Each friend picked up the string and held it. Can you picture this? 50 people on each side of the road, holding a string like an imaginary guardrail. And here came the cows, all 75 of them. As they entered the road, they saw a line of people on each side of the road, each holding the exceedingly small string. At this point, I'm not sure what went through the minds of the cows. I was a little nervous. I knew the truth: this tiny string was not going to stop a half ton side of beef. But it didn't matter what I thought, all that mattered is what the cows thought. And they bought it. They bought the lie.

I'm not sure what went through the minds of the cows that day. Maybe they thought, "I don't want to touch that string; you never know what it might do to me." Maybe another thought, "The string! I've heard stories about Uncle Ned. He touched the string once and never was right after that." Maybe some of the calves thought, "No adult cow in his right mind is getting close to that death string. No way I'm going near it."

Regardless of what the cows were thinking that day, I know this: They believed the lie. Think about it; any one of those cows could have walked through the string and escaped. The string would have been powerless against them; except, they didn't see the string. They saw a lie, the stronghold. We moved approximately 75,000 pounds of cattle with a lie.

Our thoughts do the same to us. Strongholds are lies which cause us to walk in a direction that we may not intend. If the cows had identified the stronghold, it would have been a game changer. What if one of the smarter cows stopped and really started to think. I imagine Benny the cow (You know Benny? Smarter than the

> Strongholds are lies which cause us to walk in a direction that we may not intend.

average cow. Always winning at Scrabble. He's not much for Facebook but loves to read medical journals and philosophy). Imagine Benny standing on his back two legs and addressing his fellow cows. "Friends, why are we going wherever these humans tell us? Yes, there is a string. But I'm here to say the string has no power. Don't let it lie to you. It won't hurt. It won't sting. Walk - or run - right through it." Had Benny spoken up, the cows (and the string holders) would have had quite a different day.

In order to break a stronghold, you have to identify the stronghold. What is the *string* that is lying to you? It is here that we have to do some hard internal work, but the formula is simple. In order to find the stronghold, we repeatedly ask ourselves the "Why?" questions.

For example, sometimes my battle comes on Saturday night (the day before I preach). My mind races. I stop and think and ask myself: What is the emotion I am feeling? In this case, it is anxiety. Now that I have the emotion, I need to identify the stronghold. To do that, I keep asking, "Why?" It goes something like this.

Question: **Why** are you anxious?

Answer: I am speaking in front of a bunch of people.

Question: **Why** does that make you anxious?

Answer: Something may go wrong. I could forget what I was saying. I could slip and say a bad word. I could bore people. I could make them mad.

Question: **Why** does any of that matter?

Answer: It could cause me to look incompetent.

Question: **Why** does it matter?

Answer: I don't want to look foolish.

Question: **Why** does *that* matter?

Answer: I want people to like me.

Question: **Why** do you want people to like you?

Answer: If people don't like me, I have no value to them, to God, or to myself.

Boom! At this point, we have identified the stronghold: my value as a person is determined by my performance. (Let that sink in. I think many of us may live here.) When you identify the stronghold, you can see how ridiculous it is. Kind of like a string and a cow.

TRUTH THE STRONGHOLD

Now that we have determined the emotion and identified the stronghold, we are ready for war. This is not physical, but it is sometimes more intense: a war against the powers that want to come and change our minds (Ephesians 6:12). Why? The enemy knows that if we are transformed by the renewal of our minds, he can cripple us by the destruction of our minds. It's war time, and this is where it gets fun.

> "*We demolish arguments* and *every pretension* that sets itself up against the knowledge of God, and we take captive every thought to make it obedient to Christ" (Romans 10:5; emphasis mine).

What is the best way to fight a lie? Simple: with truth. Had the cows known the truth of the string, they would have been free. When we apply the truth to a stronghold, we can be free. Where do we find the truth? We find truth in two different places: (1) Jesus, (2) the Bible.

Jesus makes a bold claim about Himself. When explaining to his followers who He is, He said "... I am the way and the *truth* and the life. ..." (John 14:6; emphasis mine).

To eliminate strongholds, we apply the Truth (Jesus) to our lies. How? We invite Him in through prayer. It can be as simple as, "Jesus, I have anxiety right now, and I believe that my performance is equal to my value, so I am inviting You, the Truth, to come into that battle." Have you invited Jesus the Truth into your battle, or are you trying to fight it on your own? He created our minds, so He knows exactly what we need in order to break the stronghold.

A second place we find truth is in scripture. Our Bible is a book of truth. Hundreds, if not thousands, of verses in the Bible tell us the truth about who we are. In order to "truth" a stronghold, we take a truth in scripture and apply it to the lie. For example, let's say we have identified that we have a stronghold of low self-esteem, and we feel of little value (we think that we are unintelligent, ugly, overweight, unpopular, and unwanted). We smash truth on that stronghold with a scripture like Psalm 139 which says . . .

"I praise you because I am fearfully and wonderfully made; your works are wonderful, I know that full well" (Psalm 139:14).

The truth of Psalm 139:14 is that we are wonderful. How do we know? Because God's works are wonderful. We are His work. Therefore, we are wonderful. So, we "truth" the stronghold by looking in the mirror and saying (maybe even out loud):

"Hello, wonderful. You are created by God. Everything that He makes is wonderful, and, since He made me, I am wonderful. Others may believe differently, but I know the truth."

The truth of who we are is found all over scripture. By reading, saying, praying, and believing truth, we break apart strongholds. The power of scripture is like nothing else we can imagine. Without its truth in our lives, we will be trapped by the stronghold. We will stay in the ditch. But, when we break apart a stronghold with truth, we find freedom.

We can search for scriptures through a physical Bible, through the internet, or several apps, including YouVersion. (YouVersion currently has a search feature where you can search "What the Bible says about . . .")

> When we break apart a stronghold with truth, we find freedom.

Let's dig a little deeper on this idea of smashing strongholds with truth. Our enemy, the devil, is a sly one. Because he wants to darken our minds, he will often be subtle in his approach. One of his tricks is to tell us a lie mixed with a little truth. Paul mentions this in Romans when he uses the term "pretension:"

> "We demolish arguments and *every pretension* that sets itself up against the knowledge of God, and we take captive every thought to make it obedient to Christ" (Romans 10:5; emphasis mine).

Paul tells us that we not only demolish arguments, but we also demolish "pretensions." What is the difference? Webster's dictionary defines a "pretension" as a ". . . claim or effort to establish a claim."[3] Said another way, a pretension is a statement or thought that is *pretending* to be true. An example:

Several years ago, I was fortunate to travel with my family to Australia. We arrived in Sydney completely jet lagged due to the 16-hour time change. As we settled into the hotel, our then seven-year-old Maddy, fell asleep on the bed. It was 7:00 p.m. Wanting to have some fun (and maybe still spacey from the time travel), we decided to play a bit of a prank on Maddy. I went to the bed and started to gently wake her. "Hey, it's time to get up. It's 7:30 in the morning. You fell asleep in your clothes." She looked at the clock. She read the time: 7:30. "You have been sleeping forever and we are ready to start the day." She rubbed some sleep from her eyes and even mumbled something like, "Man, that was a short night." We persuaded her to clean herself up. She gathered her stuff, and we walked out of the room. We made it as far as the hotel lobby before I laid the truth on her. She had not slept all night. She had slept about 30 minutes.

How did I get Maddy from the bed to the lobby? I gave her a pretension, a statement that was *pretending* to be true. I did not completely lie when I told her it was 7:30. I just didn't tell her that it was 7:30 *p.m.*

Our enemy does the same to us. He will dress up his attack with a partial truth. By doing so, it helps his statement to be more believable. He thinks it makes us more sus-ceptible to his lies. Not anymore As we figure out his ways, we can put truth on the pretensions.

Often when the enemy uses pretension, he also uses an accusation. This makes sense because another name for Satan is "the accuser of our brothers and sisters" (Revelation 12:10). Knowing who he is (accuser) and how he operates (pretension) gives us a leg up on destroying his lies. As an accuser and one who uses pretension, we know what to look for. Here are a few examples of how our enemy uses accusation and pretension. (Remember, a pretension is a lie pretending to be a fact).

Accusation: You will never graduate because you are so dumb that you are struggling with the class.

Truth: You are struggling with a class.

Pretension: You will never graduate because of a class struggle.

Accusation: You are single because nobody finds you valuable enough to love.

Truth: You are single.

Pretension: Because you are single, you are not valued.

Accusation: Your kids are acting out because you are a terrible parent and have no idea what you are doing.

Truth: My kids are acting out. I have no idea what I am doing.

Pretension: I am a terrible parent.

Truth is the most powerful weapon we have against strongholds. We find truth in Jesus. We find truth in His Word. When we apply the truth, we destroy the arguments and pretensions of the enemy. I think I already hear him whimpering.

> Truth is the most powerful weapon we have against strongholds.

Once we have attacked the stronghold with truth, the fight is not over. Most of these battles are not a "one-and-done-event." Typically, when we start to destroy strongholds with truth, shrapnel will fly. The enemy will regroup for another attack. No worries. We will be ready. Which leads us to our next phase; we capture every thought.

CAPTURE EVERY THOUGHT

"We demolish arguments and every pretension that sets itself up against the knowledge of God, and we *take captive every thought* to make it obedient to Christ" (Romans 10:5; emphasis mine).

We have **D**etermined the emotion, **I**dentified the stronghold, and **T**ruthed the stronghold. It is at this point that we can expect another attack. Our enemy may lob "thought grenades" at us. He does this in hopes that the thoughts will take root in our minds, form unhealthy pathways, and begin to unravel all the work that we have done. We fight against spiritual forces that are both crafty and unrelenting. Be ready for another round.

When the negative or unproductive thoughts arise, immediately capture them. This is not an optional "do-it-if-you-feel-like-it" scenario. This is a life and death fight, a capture-or-be-captured moment. Our thoughts will make a play to throw us back in prison. However, instead of our thoughts dragging us away and taking us captive, we are going to reverse the play and take them captive.

In order to capture thoughts, we have to think about what we are thinking about. The mind is an amazing creation that sometimes seems to run itself. Left to its own, it can wander down some dark and treacherous paths. But God has given us the ability to direct our minds. We can stop and think about what we are thinking about. How amazing!

When our minds wander in the wrong direction, we stop and take that thought in hand. At this point we often make a critical mistake. We capture the thought and hold onto it. And we stop.

> In order to capture thoughts, we have to think about what we are thinking about.

On occasion my father, my brother, and I will take a fishing trip to Canada. While in the Great White North, we spend some quality time on the water, secretly hoping to pull in a trophy fish. While we have yet to land one for the record books, we typically have enough to make some fantastic meals (and some great memories). Typically, we fish Northern Pike and Walleye. The Northern is a fantastic fish for sport. They are strong, big, and typically put up an energetic fight. Once these bad boys are in the boat, they are still in the angry phase. As they flip and flop, we grab them with a hand. They have been captured. But they are still alive and fighting hard to get free. Their next stop is either on a stringer or in a gunny sack, but, what if all we did was capture a fish, grab it in hand, and hold on to it for the rest of the day?

Can you imagine walking around with a live fish in your hand? You run to pick the kids up from school, driving with one hand. You swing by and grab a pizza for dinner, walking in and feeling weird with a fish in your hand (never mind that the pizza guy wonders why you are not having fish for dinner). You get home, check the phone, get ready for bed, tuck yourself in, all with a fish in your hand. Ridiculous right?

The same is true with our thoughts. We are told to capture them, yes, but we are not to hold onto them. Paul tells us that we not only capture our thoughts, we have to put them under Christ.

"We demolish arguments and every pretension that sets itself up against the knowledge of God, and we take captive every thought to *make it obedient to Christ"* (Romans 10:5; emphasis mine).

We take the captured thoughts and we transfer their residency. The thought has to be brought under the authority of Jesus. This leads us to the final phase of our method.

HAND IT TO JESUS

"Cast all your anxiety on him because he cares for you" (1 Peter 5:7).

Rachael is a follower of Jesus and part of our staff. One Monday I walked into her office. Her face told the story. When I asked what was up, she explained to me she was under some heavy anxiety. Her teenage son was headed out on a youth group trip to Florida the next day. This mother's heart was full of worry. I assured her that he would be safe. No need to sweat it. I was confident that he would return safely (and with great memories). She was not so sure.

"I'm just worried. I had him install a tracker app on his phone and I will not sleep soundly until he comes back."

"Rachael," I said, "Are you being a little overdramatic? Is it really worth all the anxiety?

Where is this coming from?"

"Scot, when I was younger, my sister was killed in a car accident."

Rachael had some heavy worry wanting to creep in on her. Earlier that week, I had heard Pastor Craig Groeschel teach on how to practically cast our anxiety on Christ.[3] (Side note: If you are looking for some solid resources to help your spiritual walk, Pastor Craig and his church (Life Church) produce solid spiritual content and have impacted millions of people). Fresh from Pastor Craig's teaching, I wanted to implement his idea.

I left my office and got a box, a sharpie, and a 3x5 card. I returned to Rachael's office. "OK, Rach. If you want to kill this worry, I have something that may help." I handed her a box. On the outside of the box I wrote "God" with the sharpie. Under it, I wrote "1 Peter 5:7" I also handed her a 3x5 card. She looked at me a little puzzled.

"Here is the deal. Take the box. Put it somewhere other than your bedroom. When you lie down at night and start to worry, get out of bed. Go find the 3x5 card and write your worry on your card. As an act of casting your anxiety

> As an act of casting your anxiety on Him, place your worry in the God box.

on Him, place your worry in the God box. Then go back to bed. If you start to worry again and can't get past it, get up. Go to the God box, take the card out of the box, and tell God that you are taking it back because He can't handle it."

Rachael will not tell you that she slept like a baby that week, but she did report that her anxiety was lower because she captured her thoughts and gave them to God. Maybe we would all do well to grab a box, a sharpie, and a 3x5 card.

We need to stop owning these thoughts that come into our minds. It is time we hand them to a new owner. Jesus wants our anxiety. I picture Him standing in front of us, motioning with His hands, as if to say, "Come on. Let me have those worries. You were never supposed to carry them. Your enemy laid those on you. I'll take it from here. You go and live with peace."

Remember my terrible Saturday night? The one where the anxiety chased me hard? I woke up the next morning with some fire in my bones. Tired of living under the lies, I decided it was time to fight. I sat down, asked God to lead me, and worked my stress through the DITCH system. I took my pen to paper and wrote down everything I could think of. I determined the emotion, identified the stronghold, truthed the stronghold, captured the thoughts, and handed them to Jesus. The result? Freedom. The process is continual, but I know this: We *can* be transformed by the renewal of our minds (Romans 12:2). When we change our thinking, we change our lives.

> When we change our thinking, we change our lives.

I know you can be changed. Freedom is here for the taking. In the following chapters, we will dig into some of the most common emotions we experience. We will apply the DITCH method to the emotions, and then we will look at what the Bible has to say about using those emotions for good.

Let's get to it!

DITCH

Determine the emotion

Identify the stronghold

Truth the stronghold

Capture thoughts

Hand it to Jesus

1.5

Redeem

**Ditching our negative emotions
and letting God do his work**

In the following chapters, we will run the most common emotions through the DITCH method. In addition (and here is where it gets fun), we will look at how God uses our emotions for good. Emotions like:

- Anger
- Annoyance
- Sadness
- Guilt
- Fear/Anxiety
- Discouragement
- Apathy
- Disappointment

Here is the crazy truth: God uses everything for His good. Our anger, discouragements, sadness, all of it. He can turn anything for good. Listen to this:

"And we know that in all things God works for the good of those who love him, who have been called according to his purpose" (Romans 8:28).

I love that promise. If you love Him (I bet you do), and if you have been called by Him (I bet you have, and, if not, contact me and let's get that sorted out), then God works everything for your good. I did a study on the word "everything." You know what it means? It means "everything" (brilliant, I know). So then, if He works everything for our good, He can work our anger for our good. He can work our annoyance for our good. He can work sadness, guilt, anxiety, discouragement, apathy, and disappointment for our good. Does that fire you up? What the enemy wants to use in order to tear you down, God wants to use in order to build you up. It's the same thing He did for a guy named Joseph in the Old Testament. Joseph put it like this:

> What the enemy wants to use in order to tear you down, God wants to use in order to build you up.

"You intended to harm me, but God intended it for good to accomplish what is now being done, the saving of many lives" (Genesis 50:20).

Put on your seatbelt. This is going to be a fun ride. Together, we will look at how we can DITCH what the enemy meant for evil, and we will learn how God wants to use our emotions for the ultimate good.

Let's go!

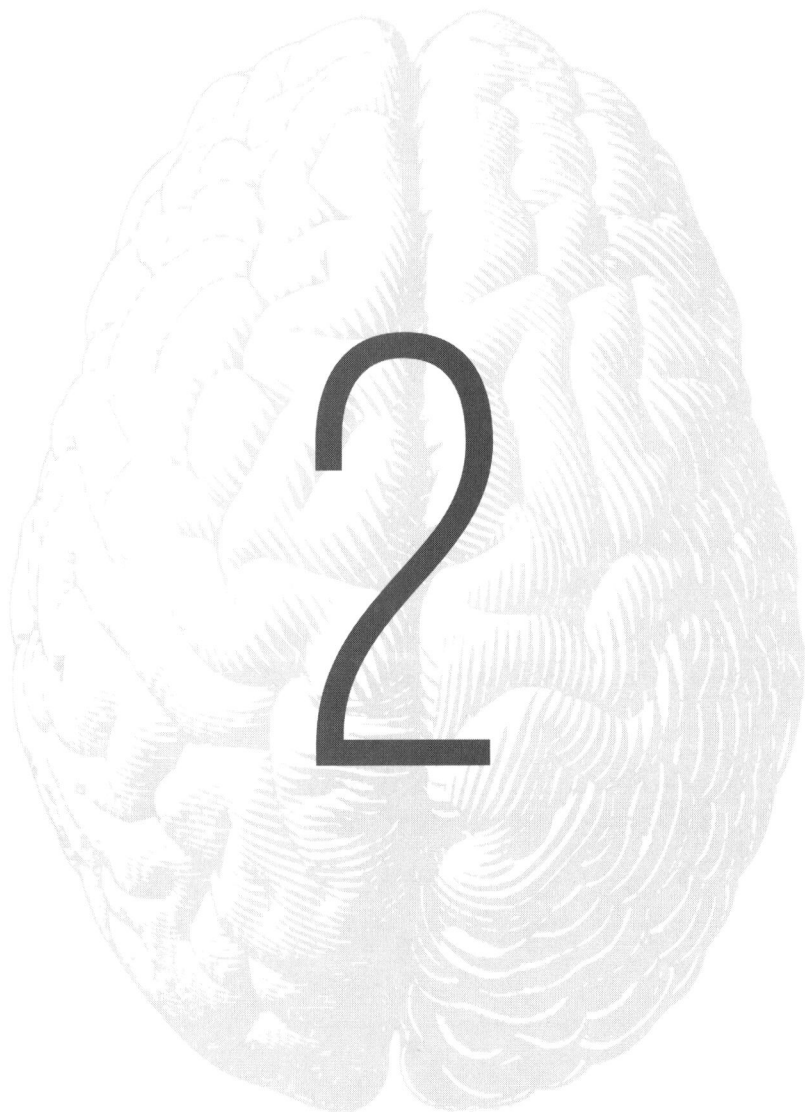

2

DITCH the Anger

DETERMINE THE EMOTION

I'm not sure what she said to me, but she had pushed my buttons. It had been a long day at work, and I was already on edge. Newly married and still trying to figure out how to navigate life together, my mind was not in the best place. Steph said something that triggered an anger in me that I didn't even know was there. She was not mean; I just didn't know how to deal with the truth she was telling me. In my anger I picked up a TV remote and threw it at the wall. Such a mature move. (I've since chilled my anger, but at times I can feel a little fire building inside.)

Easy enough, tossing a remote at a wall has helped us to determine the emotion: anger.

IDENTIFY THE STRONGHOLD

Anger is an external action of something deeper. Something inside of us is triggering this reaction. To identify the stronghold (lie) causing the anger, we ask the series of "Why?" questions.

When it comes to anger, it helps to understand that anger comes from frustration. Frustration comes from unmet expectations. This is beneficial as we start to identify the stronghold by asking the "Why?" questions.

Question: **Why** did I throw the remote?
Answer: I was frustrated.

Question: **Why** was I frustrated?
Answer: My expectations were not met.

Question: **What** expectations?
Answer: I expected to feel like a good husband.

Question: **Why** is feeling like a good husband important?
Answer: Because if I am not a good husband I am a failure.

It is here that the stronghold is becoming clear. In this case, the stronghold is that if I am a poor husband, I am a complete failure.

TRUTH THE STRONGHOLD

Once we find the stronghold (lie), we apply the truth of scripture to it. It is here that we search the Bible and find truth. (An internet search or a Bible app like YouVersion might be helpful.)

CAPTURE THOUGHTS

Once we put the smackdown on the lies that trigger anger, we expect the enemy to bring other thoughts back at us. Thoughts like . . .

- "You have a right to be angry."
- "You should give them a taste of their own medicine."

We capture those thoughts by thinking about what we are thinking about. We grab them and hold onto them.

HAND IT TO JESUS

With our captured thought in hand, we give it to Jesus. This may be as simple as a prayer or as aggressive as writing our angry thoughts and putting them in the God box (see chapter 1).

FROM ANGER TO JUSTICE

Because He works all things together for good, God will even use our anger. Left unchecked, our anger can destroy. However, when we hand our anger to God, He often does the miraculous; He directs our anger to change the world. Such was the case when my anger met a little girl named Hannah.

Mariah, my then six-year-old daughter, had saved some money and deeply desired a swing set. One Saturday we noticed a garage sale at a house on our street. At the garage sale was a used swing set. Mariah and I walked down the street, cash in hand, and talked to the owner of said swing set: a seven-year-old girl named Hannah. We traded cash for swings and took the set to our house. What we thought was a simple transaction turned out to be a life-altering event.

> What we thought was a simple transaction turned out to be a life-altering event.

In the days to come, Mariah and Hannah would spend time together. As days turned into months, we learned more about Hannah. My wife Stephanie and I started to understand Hannah and some of the challenges she experienced growing up. Her father passed away when she was very young. Life seemed to be stacked against her. Without going into detail, I will tell you that when Steph and I continued to learn about the obstacles surrounding Hannah, one emotion came straight to the surface: anger. This was not anger that made me want to throw a remote against the wall; this was an anger that made us want to resource a young lady and help her rise above her circumstances.

In our anger, Steph and I decided we would fight any injustice surrounding Hannah. She still lived with her mom, but Hannah had an open invitation to our family. She joined us on vacations. Together we navigated school, college, new jobs, breakups, makeups, and life events (like graduating college). Today, Hannah is on her own and is not a victim of injustice. Steph and I were not the only influencers in her life, but I'm sure we were part of freeing her journey. Just last week she sent me a text that read, "You saved me." It all started with a used swing set and a big dose of anger.

One of the ways that God fights injustice is through anger. As we get a handle on what makes us angry, let's not kill anger, let's kill *unproductive* anger.

> Let's not kill anger, let's kill unproductive anger.

In the Old Testament book of Nehemiah, we run across a leader named Nehemiah. This guy was becoming a world changer in his day. Nehemiah was on a mission to rebuild the protective walls around Jerusalem. The city and the people were in a mess. There was a famine, affecting the physical health of the people and creating a financial crisis for families. In the city, there were some Jews who were rich and some who were dirt poor. Some of the wealthy would lend money to their fellow Jews at high interest (this was against God's instructions in Exodus 22:25). Some Jews would even buy the children of other Jews to use them as servants. To say that Israel was full of injustice would be an understatement.

Enter Nehemiah.

> "When I heard their outcry and
> these charges, I was *very angry*"
> (Nehemiah 5:6; emphasis mine).

Nehemiah became aware of the injustice and blew a gasket. Anger rolled around in him. He was steaming. Nehemiah didn't throw a remote (or a brick from the rubble). He directed his anger toward injustice. I believe God does the same today. Could it be that He wants to use our anger and direct it toward injustice?

Side note: Let's be clear; anger is not a sin. *Misplaced* anger is a sin. Paul instructs the

Ephesians of this when he says, "'In your anger do not sin': Do not let the sun go down while you are still angry" (Ephesians 4:26).

HOW TO USE ANGER TO FIGHT INJUSTICE

If we are going to direct our anger toward injustice, we are going to need to take some specific actions. This means capturing our thoughts and handing them to Jesus so that He can turn our anger into action. Here are a few specific actions that we need to take as we use our anger to fight injustice.

1. Listen

"When I *heard* their outcry and these charges, I was very angry" (Nehemiah 5:6; emphasis mine).

Note that Nehemiah didn't get angry until he heard the outcry of the people. Had Nehemiah been stuck in his own world, he would have never heard. If he spent all of his time with his face in his phone and his ears jammed with headphones, he would have never been angry at injustice.

In 2011 I stood in a large field in Uganda, Africa. Two weeks earlier, the field had been one of the largest slums in the country. For decades the poorest of the poor had come there, built shacks, and struggled to exist. Just before our arrival, the Ugandan government had rolled in with bulldozers. They evicted 19,000 people. The shacks were leveled leaving all the people to scramble for other places to live. Hearing that story may make you sad, but it made me angry.

Standing in the field, my anger started boiling because of the injustice. I believe that my anger was so strong because I was not reading a story on the internet; I was being told the story by my African friend Richmond Wandera. Richmond told me of how he had grown up in this development. He took me to the church where he had come to know Christ and had been a sponsored child with Compassion International. With my own eyes I saw his church in ruins. Bulldozers had destroyed the structure, crushing the pulpit, pews, and dreams of church attenders. What I heard and saw that day made me angry because it was personal.

Injustice is all around us; we just need to listen. We would do well to monitor the noise in our lives. Put down the phone. Close Facebook. Pause Netflix. Listen to the conversations around you. Lean into the stories of people. Do any of their stories invoke some anger? If so, God may be wanting you to tap into anger as a fuel to curb injustice.

Once we have listened, you would think that we are ready to jump into action. Not so fast. Let's revisit our friend Nehemiah and look at what step he took.

2. Ponder

> "When I heard their outcry and
> these charges, I was very angry. I
> *pondered* them in my mind . . ."
> (Nehemiah 5:6-7; emphasis mine).

Before we jump from listening to action, we need to ponder. Why? I mean, after all, this injustice needs fixed and it needs fixed now, right? Why would we wait around? While we wait, others are being driven deeper into trouble. Doesn't it make sense that we fix the injustice now? Well, maybe. But we must be careful. We want to make sure that we are taking the right action and not just any action. Most of the time, our first plan is not always the best plan.

Especially because we are dealing with anger, we need to make sure that we allow some time

> **The initial adrenaline rush of anger can lead us to some rash actions.**

to ponder, to think deeply. This allows space for the steam of our anger to wear off. The initial adrenaline rush of anger can lead us to some rash actions that don't make a difference in the long haul. I have seen this way too many times.

On occasion, I meet someone who has looked at his own life. He has realized that he is full of sin. He is angry at his past, angry at his choices, angry at how he has treated people, angry at his sin, and is ready to make a change. I applaud the change. I celebrate the change. I'm an advocate for that change. But I want the change to be long-lasting.

Conversations with these types of people usually sound something like this:

"Man, I just accepted Christ last week. I have been doing drugs most of my life. I have been in and out of jail. I have a bunch of kids that I have not seen in a long time. Alcohol was a big problem. I'm looking for a job because the last three just didn't work out. I have a record and a warrant, but I'm working on that. Anyway, man, I just became a Christian, and God is calling me to start a church in Haiti. They don't have many churches there, and I need to fix that."

I'm not trying to be mean here, but I can just about write the next chapter of this guy's story. He will hang around church a couple more weeks and then fade away. Why? Because he did not ponder his anger. His anger should not have been on the lack of churches in Haiti. His anger should have been directed to the mess that his actions had made.

Contrast that conversation with my friend Seth. Seth showed up at our church several years ago. I caught up with him in the atrium and started a conversation. In his trademark white T-shirt, Seth was filled with nerves, feeling completely out of place. Our discussion went something like this:

"Hey, I'm Scot. What is your name?

"I'm Seth."

"Great to meet you Seth. First time here?"

"Yea, man. I'm, well, just out of jail. And this whole church deal is kind of freaking me out.

I became a Christian in jail, and I am just taking this next step. I'm really not sure what to do yet."

Over time, Seth pondered his anger and directed it where the Lord was leading. Seth joined a discipleship group, put his energy toward becoming a union electrician, and eventually saw his record expunged.

The difference between these two men is that one directed his thinking toward Jesus, while the other just did what seemed right. There is power in taking the time to stop and think. After all, if God created our minds, maybe we should stop and use them to do some deep thinking on occasion. Why? Because we want to hear the voice of God and not the voice of our own anger. Sometimes the anger creates emotion, which can lead us astray. When we stop and ponder, we let the dust of our anger settle and we are able to come up with a better plan.

Throughout scripture we see God's people get into trouble because they don't stop and think. We also see people who live amazing lives because they stop and ponder. Consider Mary, the mother of Jesus. Mary had just given

> When we stop and ponder, we let the dust of our anger settle and we are able to come up with a better plan.

birth to the Son of God. She was with Joseph, hanging around the manger, being visited by people who knew this was the Christ child. You know, just a typical day. Can you even imagine? What was going through Mary's mind? Maybe she was thinking, "We need a better place. We need to make a plan to get out of here. We need to set something in motion to tell people about Jesus." Nope. Check out what Luke says about the reaction of Mary:

> "So they hurried off and found Mary and Joseph, and the baby, who was lying in the manger. When they had seen him, they spread the word concerning what had been told them about this child, and all who heard it were amazed at what the shepherds said to them. But Mary treasured up all these things and *pondered* them in her heart" (Luke 2:16-19; emphasis mine).

There is a time for pondering. The world's greatest influencers take time to think before they take action. However, we don't want to stay in the pondering stage. After all, just thinking about something doesn't change the world. At some point, we need to take action. Back to our friend, Nehemiah. Once he pondered, he moved onto the next action.

3. Accuse

> "When I heard their outcry and
> these charges, I was very angry.
> I pondered them in my mind and
> then *accused* the nobles and
> officials. I told them, 'You are
> charging your own people interest!'
> So I called together a large
> meeting to deal with them.
> (Nehemiah 5:6-7; emphasis mine).

After Nehemiah got angry and took time to ponder, his next step was to accuse. That may seem a little out of sorts, but before we attack an injustice, we must know *where* to attack. I find it interesting that Nehemiah did not accuse the enemy. During this time period, the Jews had enemies who were doing all they could in order to not see the Jerusalem wall rebuilt. Yet, Nehemiah did not go after them. He went after the immediate source of the injustice: his fellow Jews. If Nehemiah were part of your church and he saw an injustice, he would likely get angry, ponder, and then come and accuse the people of the church.

Pause. I can hear it now. "Hey, I'm part of the church. You are not my judge. Only God judges. Don't come and confront me when you have your own mess to deal with." I have heard similar statements from Christians whenever we

> We are supposed to hold each other accountable.

talk about sin and confrontation. The fact of the matter is that we are supposed to hold each other accountable. Listen to the words of Jesus:

> "If your brother or sister sins, go and point out their fault, just between the two of you. If they listen to you, you have won them over" (Matthew 18:15).

When followers of Jesus approach me and accuse me of injustice, I may not be happy

47

about it, but I can't fault them. They are doing what scripture commands. Such was the case for me when I was young in ministry.

In the 90s, I was a full-time worship leader. Part of my responsibilities included recruiting worship team members. During one particular season, we were short on female vocalists. I looked long and hard for a vocalist that would fit our team. For whatever reason, none could be found. However, my friend who was also a worship leader in another department at our church, had a couple of tremendous vocalists on his team.

In a complete lapse of judgement, I approached one of his vocalists and asked if she would be interested in serving with our band. She informed me that she could only serve with one worship team but would consider my offer. I'm embarrassed to admit that in all of this, I did not talk to my worship-leading friend. I was about to cause him to lose a member of his team, and I didn't even have the courtesy to have a conversation with him.

My friend soon found out about my actions, and we sat down for a conversation. After pondering my actions he gracefully corrected the offender: me. And I am glad that he did.

Because of the proper accusation of my friend, I was able to see the injustice I had caused. I had "stolen" someone from his team. I was able to confess before God and before my friend. I asked for forgiveness and took action to right the wrong. This all took place a couple decades ago, and I'm happy to report that he and I are still close even to this day. I am grateful that he addressed the injustice. Oh, let's be clear; I don't like talking about the situation. I'm not thrilled to write about it, and it's not a laughing matter between my friend and me; but I am grateful for a brother who would be brave enough to accuse me. I am better for it.

As we accuse others, we need to be careful in identifying who the battle is with. In our anger, it is easy to want to decimate an individual. "Oh, they are the ones bringing on the injustice, wait until I get ahold of them. I will destroy them." Let's be cautious. Our enemy is not typically our fellow man. Our ultimate battle is not with humans. Your battle is not with me. My battle is not with you. Our ultimate target is not with those who persecute Christians, with abortion doctors, or those funding the sex trade. Our battle is with the injustice of their behavior, and behind their behavior is the father of lies, Satan himself. That's why Paul writes,

> "For our struggle is not against flesh and blood, but against the rulers, against the authorities, against the powers of this dark world and against the spiritual forces of evil in the heavenly realms" (Ephesians 6:12).

I am grateful that my friend did not want to destroy me. He wanted to destroy the darkness in me. The same is true for us. We don't struggle against our fellow humans; we struggle against the darkness behind them.

> **My friend did not want to destroy me. He wanted to destroy the darkness in me.**

Once we have listened to our anger, pondered what to do, and accused the offender, it's time to get to some action (insert big musical score. I'm hearing the A-Team theme here, but then again, I'm 100 years old).

4. Act

At this point, we are ready to take some deeper action. Some of the action may have been done in the accusation stage, but here it goes even deeper. For Nehemiah, it meant that he went public with his actions.

> "When I heard their outcry and these charges, I was very angry. I pondered them in my mind and then accused the nobles and officials. I told them, 'You are charging your own people interest!' So I *called together a large meeting* to deal with them and said: As far as possible, we have bought back our fellow Jews who were sold to the Gentiles. Now you are selling your own people, only for them to be sold back to us!' They kept quiet, because they could find nothing to say" (Nehemiah 5:6-8; emphasis mine).

Can you picture this? Nehemiah calls a meeting. Maybe they thought this was a pep rally. Maybe they were anticipating a motivational speech. Maybe they were looking for some good news. I imagine people gathering, taking a seat, getting ready for a big announcement.

I can see Nehemiah pacing back and forth, mumbling under his breath. Maybe his officials are whispering to each other, "What is up with all of this?" Another looks at him as if to say, "It's about to get ugly."

There is no pep talk to be had. Nehemiah unloads. He can't believe what the Jews are doing to each other. He doesn't mince words or soft sell what was happening. He lays it down. Probably red faced and out of breath. The response from the crowd? Silence.

Why the silence? You would think that someone would stand and make a defense. But there was no defense to be made. Why? Because every Jew knew what they were doing was wrong. Nehemiah simply verbalized what they already knew.

> When we act, our words meet conviction, and the chains of injustice begin to loosen.

When we act on injustice, many times we are bringing to light what others are already feeling. They know their actions are wrong, but they stuff it deep down inside. They think that since nobody is talking about it, it must not be that big of a deal. However, when we act, our words meet conviction, and the chains of injustice begin to loosen.

At this point, it would be easy to get a big head. After all, we have a holy anger, and we are using it to right wrongs. If we are not careful, we can foster pride and arrogance. It is interesting to note that Nehemiah had no arrogance. We read in a later verse of Nehemiah 5 that Nehemiah did all he could to share with the poor and even refuseed to take land and food that previous kings enjoyed. He would not allow himself to become one who inflicted injustice on others.

Let's be honest, friends, we can't stop injustice for the whole world. We can, however, stop injustice for some. Let's make a deal. You find the injustice that makes you angry, and I will find the injustice that makes me angry. We will listen, ponder, accuse, and act. In doing so, we will see God use our anger to make His kingdom, His church, and His people stronger.

3

DITCH the Annoyance
(weak anger)

DETERMINE THE EMOTION

"You are sooooo annoying!" As a parent, I heard my kids say this more than I would like to admit. Typically, it came with a whiny tone, mixed with desperation and a hope that the action will stop.

Do we outgrow being annoyed? To a point. Perhaps what bothers us changes as we grow older, but we still find that we are annoyed. It could be any number of actions that annoy us:

- Fingernails on a chalkboard
- Traffic
- Cold weather
- Long lines
- Gray skies
- Clutter

Or maybe something more serious:

- Lying
- People not living up to their potential
- The number on the bathroom scale
- Getting passed over for the promotion

Annoyances are sometimes big, sometimes small. Smaller annoyances can be dismissed as some-thing you don't like. For example, my friend Doug is annoyed by the smell of broccoli. I'm not sure he has a stronghold to identify, it's just that he thinks broccoli is nasty. It's a small annoyance. However, if an annoyance is big, we need to deconstruct it in order to get out of the rut.

> **Annoyances are sometimes big, sometimes small.**

For the sake of argument, let's pick a stronger annoyance like arrogance. Let's suppose, for whatever reason, arrogance gets under your skin. It doesn't make you full-on angry, but it annoys you deeply. The guy in the office, or the girl at school - the ones who always talks about themselves - they drive you crazy. You avoid talking to them; you roll your eyes when they start to tell a story. You know how their story ends. They are the heroes. According to them, they have more friends, more money, better experiences, and fewer problems than anyone. (And when they do have problems, well, it's always someone else's fault.) Just thinking about them gets you worked up. You, my friend, are annoyed by their arrogance. Let's break that down.

IDENTIFY THE STRONGHOLD

Because annoyance is the distant (and sometimes weaker) cousin of anger, it behaves somewhat the same way. Anger comes from frustration, and frustration comes from unmet expectations. In the same way, annoyance comes from some mild frustration.

Mild frustration comes from mild, unmet expectations. While not as strong as anger, we can still apply the same methods when we ask the "Why?" questions which drive us to identifying the stronghold.

> Annoyance comes from some mild frustration.

Question: ***Why*** did I get annoyed when he talked about himself?

Answer: I was frustrated.

Question: ***Why*** was I frustrated?

Answer: Because I expected something different.

Question: **What** did you expect?

Answer: I expected him to like me and it seems he likes himself better than he likes me.

Question: **Why** is it important to be liked?

Answer: Because if I am liked, then I am important.

It is here that we are starting to see the stronghold be revealed. In this case, the stronghold would be "If other people like me, I am important."

TRUTH THE STRONGHOLD

Once we find the stronghold, we apply the truth of scripture to it. It is here that we search the Bible (a computer search is great) and find the truth.

CAPTURE THOUGHTS

Once we put the smack down on the lies that trigger annoyance, we expect the enemy to bring other thoughts back at us:

"You have a right to be annoyed."

"They don't like you, why would they? You are not that likable."

We capture those thoughts by thinking about what we are thinking about. We grab them and hold onto them.

HAND IT TO JESUS

With our captured thoughts in hand, we give it to Jesus. This may be as simple as a prayer or as aggressive as writing our thoughts of annoyance on a card and putting them in the God box (see chapter 1).

ANNOYANCE USED FOR GOD

If we let our emotion of annoyance run un-checked, the result can be destructive. However, when we hand it to God, He can bring some miraculous results. Sometimese wants to use our annoyance to move us to action. The very thing that annoys us may be what God wants to use to motivate us to change something in our surroundings. Such was the case when I was annoyed with my old house.

Steph and I raised our girls in a three-bedroom, one bath house. You heard it right. Five people. One bathroom. It can be done. It was not always easy, but we made it work. The biggest drawback to the house was not the one bathroom. The biggest drawback was that the house was over 100 years old. Sure, being that old, the house was deep with character: woodwork, leaded windows, hardwood floors, and much more. But at 100 years old, she was heavy in use. 100-year-old stuff breaks down. All. The. Time. Chasing all the problems in this house was, you guessed it, annoying.

One of the biggest annoyances was the basement. The walls were made of large concrete blocks. They were neglected for years and as such, slowly turned from solid block to dust. I could literally see holes in the basement walls where, over time, the concrete turned to sand. No problem, except that these blocks were the foundation of my house. Finally, after years of neglect by previous owners and neglect by me, I decided it was time to do something.

> It was my job to protect the house from decay.

My annoyance turned to action. After all, this was my house. This is where my family lived. It was my job to protect the house from decay. So, I got to work. Somehow I would need to replace the crumbling walls in my basement. Again, not a big deal, except these walls were holding up the house. I should also point out that I had no idea how to repair a crumbling foundation.

Armed with annoyance, I consulted Google, YouTube, and the local Lowe's store. "How hard can it be?" Evidently, pretty hard. I bought a load of materials and spread them on the floor. In the pile were new bricks to replace the old ones, as well as some cement mix which would hold the new bricks in place. Turns out that the cement mix I was using to hold the new bricks dried fast: from liquid to rock in under 30 seconds. I had to mix a small batch and work like a squirrel jacked up on Mountain Dew. Turns out the quick drying cement was only one of the challenges I had to deal with.

In the worst part of the wall, about three feet up, blocks were breaking off in sizable chunks. I knew I needed to get the loose chunks out and replace them with new brick (according to the experts on YouTube). As I removed some of the crumbling brick, two large cinder blocks fell completely out of the wall. Allow me to pause so that you sense the gravity of the situation. My basement wall, which served as the foundation of my house, let loose of two large blocks. They crumbled from the wall and landed on the floor. My heart may have skipped a beat.

Have you ever experienced something in life where it all seems to go in slow motion? As the large blocks fell at my feet, I remember thinking, *"Ohhhhhhhh noooooooo!"* (Say it low and slow for dramatic effect.) While I don't have anything close to a structural engineering degree, I am smart enough to know that when you remove blocks from the middle of a wall, bad things happen. So, in my slow motion assessment of all that was happening, fearing that my entire house may fall down, I did the only thing I could think of: I bent my knees, raised my hands toward the basement ceiling, and braced for impact. I would save my house from falling.

> Have you ever experienced something in life where it all seems to go in slow motion?

"Really, Scot? Your foundation is crumbing, your entire house is about to fall down, and you think you are going to hold it up?"

Hey, I never said I was smart. And to be fair, the folks I googled said nothing about this even being a possibility.

As it would turn out, nothing shifted (except my pulse). Once the adrenaline wore off, I mixed a batch of liquid rock, put in some new block, and shored up the foundation. Crisis averted.

All of this could have been avoided if I had taken action earlier. We had lived in the house for almost 20 years. I knew the foundation needed attention, but I had neglected the upkeep. I walked past those walls every day and thought, "I need to take care of that sometime." Day after day I neglected the problem. It was not until I became annoyed at the walls that I did something about it. I realized that I had neglected my house, and now it was time to do something about it. I was annoyed at my neglect, and my annoyance turned into action.

> Are there some areas of your life that you are becoming annoyed with?

Are there some areas of your life that you are becoming annoyed with? Are there some areas that you have been neglecting? Maybe you think,

"Someday I will get to that. Someday I will have a prayer time. Someday I will start devotions again. Someday I will serve at church." The days roll on and nothing gets done. Maybe you even look around (like I did) and think, "Look at this mess. How did this happen?"

We all have areas in our lives that we neglect. I wonder if God uses annoyance to help us to focus on what we are neglecting. Let's jump back to the story of Nehemiah. We first visited Nehemiah in chapter 2 as we explored anger. As you recall, he uses his anger to fight injustice. Nehemiah now hits another emotion, finding himself not angry but annoyed.

As it turns out, Nehemiah is annoyed over the use of a room. There was an area in the house of God used to store sacred items (temple articles, oil, new wine, etc.). Somewhere along the way, the priest in charge (Eliashib) gave permission to his buddy Tobiah to use the room. Tobiah moved his household goods into the room for storage. Nehemiah felt his annoyance rise and for good reason.

Nehemiah's blood pressure spikes because a sacred space is being used as a storage closet for Tobiah. But that's not the only cause for his alarm. Previously, Nehemiah had rebuilt the wall around Jerusalem. During the reconstruction, he had an arch enemy. This foe did nothing but talk trash, make threats, and do all that he could in order to see Nehemiah fail. The enemy's name? You guessed it: Tobiah.

God is about to use Nehemiah's annoyance for good. The ultimate annoyance had less to do with a storage room and more to do with the fact that the house of God was neglected. Listen to Nehemiah as he points out the source of his annoyance.

> "So I rebuked the officials and asked
> them, '*Why is the house of God
> neglected?*' Then I called them together
> and stationed them at their posts"
> (Nehemiah 13:11; emphasis mine).

Like Nehemiah, God will sometimes use annoyance to motivate us to protect our spiritual house. If you feel your spiritual game has been neglected and that realization is annoying you, I have some good news: You can protect your spiritual house by taking action.

FROM ANNOYANCE TO PROTECTING THE HOUSE

Let's take a look at what we can learn from our friend Nehemiah. Under the influence of annoyance and the influence of God, Nehemiah took four actions in order to protect the house.

Action #1: Get Peeved

"I was greatly displeased and threw all Tobiah's household goods out of the room"* (Nehemiah 13:8; emphasis mine).

We have already spent much time here, but I'll say it again. Change usually starts with us being annoyed at our surroundings. Tony Robbins says it like this: "Change happens when the pain of staying the same is greater than the pain of change."[4] Before we change, we must be restlessly annoyed. If we are "»okay with our spiritual life, we probably have an "okay" spiritual life. Only when we get a little peeved are we

> **Tony Robbins says it like this: "Change happens when the pain of staying the same is greater than the pain of change."**

motivated to change. Annoyance has the ability to bring about great results. J. Willard Marriott once said it like this: "Dissatisfaction is the basis of progress."[6]

Several years ago, I found myself annoyed with my connection to Jesus. I tried reading devotional books, reading sections of the Bible, listening to worship music, praying, and ten other actions. Nothing seemed to work (and as a Pastor, you would think that this should be easy). I was annoyed, but I was not defeated. I knew that there was something out there, so I kept my eyes open for anything that would help me protect my spiritual house. Enter my friends Kim and Bob.

Kim and Bob had been a part of our church before moving to Hawaii. Once they settled in paradise, they began attending New Hope Christian Fellowship, led by Pastor Wayne Cordeiro. Pastor Wayne had developed a simple system of daily Bible reading called *Life Journaling.* Bob and Kim thought life journaling was the greatest thing since sliced bread. They told me all about it and even explained to me how to journal. Frequently my phone calls with them would start with "Hey Scot, have you tried

Life Journaling yet? It is so good. No? Oh, you *have* to try it." They followed up with emails, encouraging - almost badgering me to try this system. They even went as far as to mail a physical journal to me, all the way from Hawaii. Finally, I relented.

I tried Life Journaling for a couple reasons: One, to get Kim and Bob off my back. I figured if I tried it and it didn't work (like everything else), I would be able to say, "Well, I gave it a try, and it just doesn't work for me." The second reason

> **My annoyance spurred action.**

I gave it a try was because I was annoyed with my connection to the Lord. My annoyance spurred action.

As it turns out, Life Journaling became the lifeblood of my relationship with the Lord. This simple system of reading some scripture and writing some thoughts has brought me closer to Jesus than anything else I have done. If you looked through my journals, you would see thousands of entries, each of them representing a time when I paused and connected with the Lord through scripture and prayer. Today, I teach others to Life Journal and even require it for our church staff. I have seen loads of people have their spiritual lives rocked by this simple system, and it all started when a friend's encouragement met my annoyance.

Never underestimate the power of annoyance. The Lord may be using it so that you can get the house back in order.

Side note: I talk about how to Life Journal in my previous book, *Soul Coma* (available at scotlongyear.com). You will also find information, including a video, explaining the entire process at www.mccth.org.

Once we have recognized that we are peeved (annoyed), just like Nehemiah, we move to our second action.

Action #2: Purge

According to the Oxford dictionary, to "purge" means to "remove . . . from an organization or place in an abrupt or violent way."[7]

> This was exactly what Nehemiah did. He went violent on Tobiah's items. *"I was greatly displeased and threw all Tobiah's household goods out of the room"* (Nehemiah 13:8; emphasis mine).

I can picture Nehemiah, stepping into the room, still annoyed. He looks around in disgust. Instead of seeing the room filled with sacred items, he sees furniture, maybe some pots and pans, and piles of unused items. To make matters worse, these items belong to his enemy. Nehemiah grabs the items and violently throws them out of the room. Onlookers probably thought that he lost his mind, but it was just the opposite. He was protecting the house by removing what did not belong.

You and I must do the same. If we are going to protect our spiritual house, we need to rid it of anything that doesn't belong. Our lives are full of thoughts, actions, relationships, entertainment choices, language, and a thousand other items. How do we know what to throw out and what to keep? Simple: We ask, "Who owns this?"

As Nehemiah was going through the room, I would surmise that he picks up an item and asks, "Who does this belong to?" He picks up a jar of oil. Someone says, "Nehemiah, that oil is used by the priests and belongs to the house of God." Good. It stays. Perhaps Nehemiah picks up a bowl with utensils. "Who does this belong to"? What stays and what goes?

The same is true in our lives. As we take stock of what needs to stay or go, we need to ask, "Who owns this?" If tempted by pornography, I have to ask, "Who owns this?" It is the same with lust, greed, and gossip. We also have other items in life: relationships, entertainment, recreation, and more. Not everything needs to

"Who owns this?"

go, but not everything needs to stay. Whatever belongs to the enemy gets thrown out. But how do we determine ownership? We ask a simple question: Does this bring life, or does it bring death? Jesus says,

> "The thief comes only to steal and kill and destroy; I have come that they may have life, and have it to the full" (John 10:10).

The thief (Satan) brings death, but Jesus brings life. So, we look at everything in our lives. If it brings life, it is owned by Jesus. It stays. If it brings death, it is owned by Satan. It goes.

- Pornography? It brings death. Purge it.
- Bitterness? Death. It has to go.
- Unforgiveness? Death. Gone.

- Anger? Death. Evicted.
- Relationships? Depends.
- Recreation? Depends.
- Love? It brings life. It stays.
- Joy? Life. Keep it around.
- Church? Life. Hang onto it.

And the list goes on.

The point is this: In order to protect the house, we need to take out the trash. And, let's not be fooled into thinking that we can keep the trash around. It *must* go.

Sometimes I will get on a health kick. It usually lasts a week or two. My intentions are good, and the journey always starts the same. I tell myself I am going to eat better, then I purge the cabinets. I rid myself of everything that can bring death. Brownies, cookies, snacks, chips, twinkies – you know, basically anything good. They must go. If they stick around, they will end up in my mouth. Sometimes you just have to purge.

> **In order to protect the house, we need to take out the trash.**

What is the Lord asking you to purge? Chances are, what you purge is tied to your annoyance. If you are annoyed with the source of your sin, purge it. Annoyed with your connection with the Lord? Purge whatever is blocking your time with him. Annoyed with the tension between you and a friend? Purge it by having a conversation.

Once we have purged what brings death, we follow the example of Nehemiah and roll into our next step.

Action #3: Purify

> "I was greatly displeased and threw all Tobiah's household goods out of the room. *I gave orders to purify the rooms*, and then I put back into them the equipment of the house of God, with the grain offerings and the incense" Nehemiah 13:8-9 (emphasis mine).

It was not enough for Nehemiah that the room was empty of Tobiah's junk. The room needed to be purified. In the time of Nehemiah, purifying was a big deal. Purifying *this* room was significant. It would take more than sweeping the floor and diffusing some oils. The room was spiritually dirty, and it needed to be spiritually clean (much like our lives). It is likely that Nehemiah purified the room according to the guidelines of purification.

The ritual of purification is found in Numbers 19. To start the ritual, a bull was to be slaughtered and burned. Once fully burned, the ashes were collected, then stored in a ceremonially clean area. When it was time for a ceremonial cleansing, ashes were gathered and combined with water. Purification came from the ashes of a blood sacrifice combined with water. Blood and water are tied to purification. See any connection?

> **We are purified by the blood sacrifice of Jesus.**

We are purified by the blood sacrifice of Jesus. We are also instructed to join in the ordinance of baptism (The Greek word for baptism means to be "dipped, dunked, or immersed.").[8] Nehemiah knew that this sacred space (like our lives) would not need to be only clean and tidy, it would need to be purified.

The only way we can put our spiritual house in order is by being purified. We are not capable of purifying ourselves from sin. Only God can forgive sin. He has chosen to forgive our sin and cleanse us because of the blood sacrifice of His son Jesus. The Bible assures us of this when it says . . .

"If we confess our sins, he is faithful and just and will forgive us our sins and purify us from all unrighteousness"(1 John 1:9).

Have you been purified from your sins? Maybe your annoyance has led you to this point. Maybe you have tried to clean up on your own, but you still find yourself annoyed. If so, it's because we can't purify the house on our own. We can't take away our sins. Only the blood sacrifice of Jesus can erase the consequences of our actions. Have you asked Him to purify you? Have you asked Him to be the leader and forgiver of your life? If not, you can do that right now. And if you do, your next step is to jump into a healthy church and be baptized. Send me an email (scot@scotlongyear.com), and I will get some resources that will lead you in the right direction.

> Only the blood sacrifice of Jesus can erase the consequences of our actions.

Action #4: Put back

Nehemiah now had a clean room. He removed all the sacred items and all of Tobiah's junk. The room was purified. But he was not yet ready to put items back in the room. He was careful to put back only the items that belonged. After all, this is a holy space and only holy items are to be stored there.

> "I was greatly displeased and threw all Tobiah's household goods out of the room *I gave orders to purify the rooms*, and then I put back into them the equipmentof the house of God, with the grain offerings and the incense" (Nehemiah 13:8-9; emphasis mine).

Nehemiah only put sacred equipment back in the sacred house. All purged items were thrown out. The room was now full of items that spoke of God and his greatness.

Maybe you have made an effort to purge everything bad out of your life. While that is a noble step, it is also dangerous. When we strip everything out of our lives, including the Lord, we are in a dangerous place.

> "When an impure spirit comes out of a person, it goes through arid places seeking rest and does not find it. Then it says, 'I will return to the house I left. When it arrives, it finds the house unoccupied, swept clean and put in order. Then it goes and takes with it seven other spirits more wicked than itself, and they go in and live there. And the final condition of that person is worse than the first. That is how it will be with this wicked generation"
> (Matthew 12:43-45).

Cleaning up our lives may help in the short term, but it will do nothing to move us closer to Jesus. In fact, it may be even more harmful. Our past addictions and habits will come back and tempt us. Because we don't have the power of God working in us, we have no ability to fight, so the addiction moves back in. Lust rings the doorbell. Gossip shows up with a packed suitcase. These unsacred items are back. And with no one to fight them off, they settle in as if they are home.

We were not made to be a house of death. Our spiritual house was designed to be full of life. The only way we have life is when we invite God to move in. Good news: God and his son Jesus want to live *in* you.

> "Jesus replied, 'Anyone who loves me will obey my teaching. My Father will love them, and we will come to them and make our home with them'" (John 14:23).

> **If the Holy Spirit can raise a man from the dead, that is the kind of power I want living in my house. I bet you do as well.**

The Father and Son will make their home with us. All we have to do is ask. And as we do, He gives us the gift of the Holy Spirit. This is the same Holy Spirit that raised Christ from the dead (Romans 8:11). If the Holy Spirit can raise a man from the dead, that is the kind of power I want living in my house. I bet you do as well.

Let's be honest, all of us allow our spiritual houses to crumble. Because the Lord loves us, He will sometimes make us annoyed at the rubble. He will cause us to want to take action. When we do, we allow ourselves to get peeved, we purge anything that does not bring life, we purify our lives, and we put back the things of God.

Stop walking past the rubble. Allow your annoyance to turn to action. When you do, you will discover a life that is beyond anything you could hope for or imagine (Ephesians 3:20).

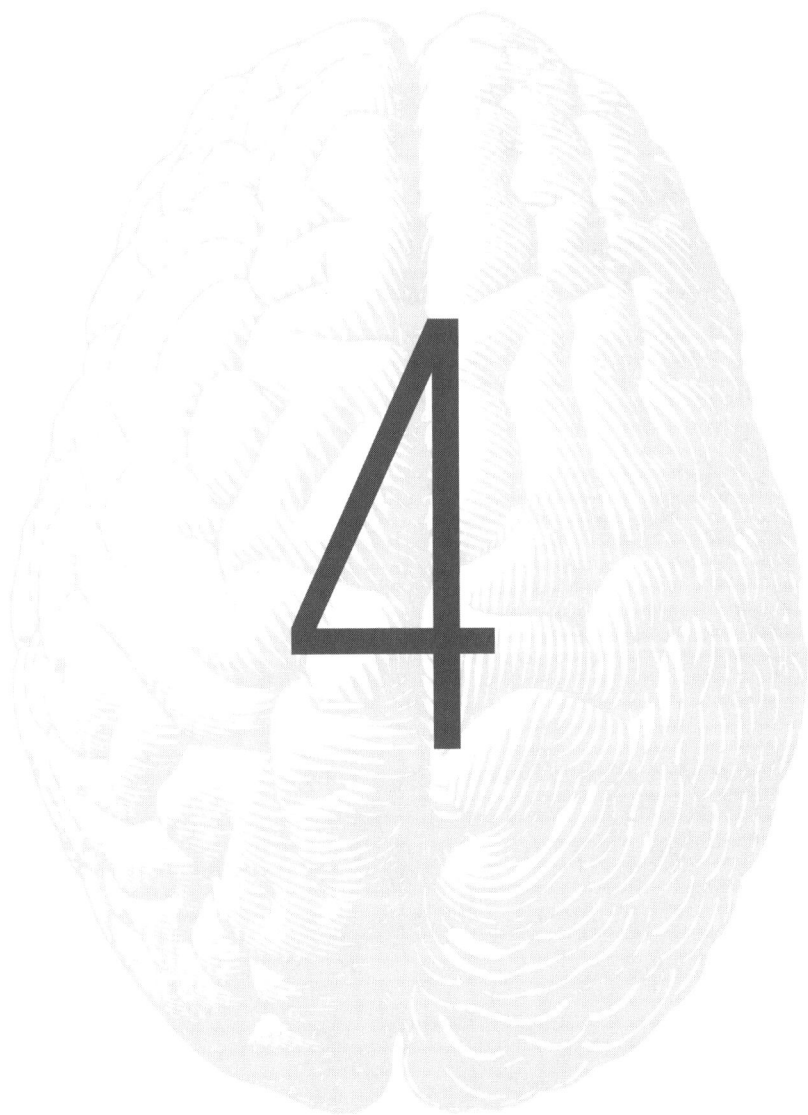

4

DITCH the Sadness

DETERMINE THE EMOTION

We were close friends. We shared much of our lives with each other. Our families would gather. My friend and I prayed together, travelled together, dreamed together, and even cried together. We shared our struggles and wins. We would laugh, the kind of laughs that would make your sides hurt, your eyes water, and everyone in the restaurant look at you like something was wrong.

When I was down, he lifted me up. When he was down, I lifted him up. I remember thinking how grateful I was to have a friend like this. A friendship to last a lifetime. Except, it did not. Our friendship drifted. Small at first, but further and further as time went by. We still talk on occasion. There is no bad blood between us, but it is not the same. Our friendship lost what it once was. And for that, I am sad.

Sadness can be weak or strong. It can be inconvenient or debilitating. Either way, if we want to DITCH the sadness, we need to dig past the pain and get some answers.

IDENTIFY THE STRONGHOLD

> More times than not, sadness is tied to a loss of some kind.

More times than not, sadness is tied to a loss of some kind. It may be the loss of a loved one, the loss of a relationship, or the loss of a job. Sometimes, it is connected to something yet to be identified. As we start deconstructing the sadness, we again ask the "Why?" questions in order to see if there is a stronghold we need to address. Note: There may or may not be a stronghold connected to sadness. For example, sadness at a loss of a loved one is a natural and healthy response and part of the grief process.

Using the example of being sad because of the loss of a friendship, let's ask the "Why?" questions:

Question: **Why** am I sad?

Answer: Because I miss the friendship.

Question: **Why** do you miss the friendship?

Answer: Because I miss someone who understood me.

Question: **Why** was that important?

Answer: With no one to understand me, I feel alone and unwanted

Question: Are you alone and unwanted by everyone (including God)?

Answer: Well . . .

Through these questions we have identified the stronghold: In this case the stronghold is, "I am alone and unwanted by everyone, including God."

TRUTH THE STRONGHOLD

Once we find the stronghold, we apply the truth of scripture to it. It is here that we search the Bible and find truth. In this case, the stronghold is that we are alone and unwanted by everyone.

CAPTURE THOUGHTS

In predictable fashion, once we put truth on

the lie, the enemy will come back with more lies. He lies so much that he is given the name "Father of Lies" (John 8:44). What a chump. He may whisper:

- "Your other friends really don't like you either; they are just being nice."
- "Good luck finding another friendship like that."
- "No wonder he left, you were not a good friend to him."

Remember, we capture those thoughts by thinking about what we are thinking about. We grab them and hold on to them.

HAND IT TO JESUS

With our captured thought in hand, we give it to Jesus. This may be as simple as a prayer like, "God, I am giving You my sadness. Thank You for wanting to take it." It may be as intense as writing our thoughts of sadness and putting them in the God box (see chapter 1).

FROM SADNESS TO INFLUENCE

What is making you sad? It may be a relationship, a rejection, or an injustice. Sadness usually comes from loss. Some losses (like death) we cannot change. However, some losses we can influence. If we have a loss of a friendship, we can re-engage that friendship. If we have the loss of a job, we can get another. Sometimes sadness fuels us to change the very thing that makes us sad. In order to change a situation, we will need to become influencers.

Think of it like this:
- I am sad.
- I am sad because of a situation.
- Can I change the situation?
- If "yes," what will I need to do?
  I will need to influence the situation.

Thus, *sadness* can launch us into *influence.* This was the case with our friend Nehemiah. (You know, this Nehemiah character is getting some major traction in this book. I feel like I need to send him a thank-you note or a Starbucks gift-card).

> Thus, sadness can launch us into *influence.*

At one point in his story, Nehemiah decided that he could be sad, or he could be an influencer. Guess what he chose? Wait, I'm getting ahead of myself. Let's dive into the story of Nehemiah again.

Nehemiah has the job of being a "cupbearer" to the king. His primary job is to taste wine for the king, making sure it is good enough for royalty. If it was bad wine, the king didn't get it. If it was poison, Nehemiah could die, and the king would be spared. (I can't imagine the life insurance rates for this kind of job.)

As Nehemiah was serving at the king's pleasure, he received word the walls around Jerusalem were broken down. The destruction of walls around a city is a big deal. Big enough that it impacted Nehemiah in an interesting way.

> "In the month of Nisan in the twentieth year of King Artaxerxes, when wine was brought for him, I took the wine and gave it to the king. I had not been *sad* in his presence before, so the king asked me, 'Why does your face look so *sad* when you are not ill? This can be nothing but *sadness* of heart.' I was very much afraid" (Nehemiah 2:1-2; emphasis mine).

Looking at this situation in Jerusalem, Nehemiah was struck with sadness. So much so, that even King Artaxerxes noticed. Nehemiah told the king the cause of his sadness:

> "but I said to the king, 'May the king live forever! Why should my face not look sad when the city where my ancestors are buried lies in ruins, and its gates have been destroyed by fire?'" (Nehemiah 2:3)

At this point, the king asked Nehemiah a pivotal question. The answer to this question determined the future of Nehemiah and the future of Jerusalem.

> "The king said to me, 'What is it you want?' . . ." (Nehemiah 2:4).

Nehemiah might have replied a hundred different ways. He could have said . . .

- "I just need some time off to clear my head."
- "I just need you to not ask me questions."
- "I just need to not have this stressful job."
- "I just need to hide in bed and sleep for a few days."

Not the case with Nehemiah. When Nehemiah answered the question, he answered as someone who is stricken with sadness but driven toward influence. God turned Nehemiah's sadness into influence. God can do the same with our sadness. To move from being sad to being an influencer, we follow the actions of Nehemiah.

FROM SADNESS TO INFLUENCE: 4 STEPS

Step #1: Pray

The king turned to Nehemiah and asked him what he wanted. Instead of spouting off a list of resources he needed, Nehemiah took a deep breath and did something unexpected.

"The king said to me, 'What is it you want?'
Then I prayed to the God of heaven"
(Nehemiah 2:4).

> The first step from sadness to influence didn't start with a plan; it started with a prayer.

For Nehemiah, the first step from sadness to influence didn't start with a plan; it started with a prayer. Nehemiah knew the source of influence is from God. He knew he didn't have what it took to get the job done. Note to whom he prayed. He didn't pray to himself. He did not ask friends for some "good vibes" or "good thoughts." He didn't consult another human. He called out to the God of heaven. If you are going to call out, you might as well go to the top.

What do you think Nehemiah prayed? We are not exactly sure, but I bet it was something like, "God, if I am going to influence, I need to get the king on board. For him to be on board, I need to use my words, so if you could not make me sound like my mouth is full of gibberish, that would be great." Or he may have prayed a prayer that I offer with frequency, "God, help!" Either way, Nehemiah prayed that his words were clear. I get it; much is won or lost based on our words, especially in critical conversations.

I had one such critical conversation when I was in high school. One evening, I slipped away to an upstairs bedroom to use the phone. Allow me to explain for our younger readers. In those days, kids, our phones were not portable. They were attached to the wall. To place a phone call (texting had not yet been invented), you would need to pick up a receiver. The receiver was connected via a curly cord to the phone. The phone itself was connected to the wall, meaning you could only go as far as your phone cord would reach. (If you were a person of means, you would have a very long cord, enabling you to hide in a bathroom and have a private conversation. A chat room of sorts.) Once you picked up the receiver, you would need to dial the phone number. Again, if you were upper crust you would have a push button phone. We (the lower of the crust) had a rotary phone, making the imputing of the digits all the more time consuming.

This particular evening, I was about to pick up the phone and dial seven digits that had the potential of changing my life. On the other end of the numbers was a girl. I decided that I was sad without her and wanted to ask her on a date. I'm pretty sure I prayed before I picked up the phone. It was critical that I *influence* this girl. So, I went straight to the top. "God, help!"

> **I was about to pick up the phone and dial seven digits that had the potential of changing my life.**

Someone picked up the phone at the other end. I'm sure my voice cracked. "Is Stephanie there?" Somehow, God heard my prayers. My sadness kicked into influence. We had a critical, life-changing conversation. I'm not sure why Stephane said yes to a date, or more dates, or marriage, but I am glad she did. Two kids and three decades later, we are still together.

To move toward influence, we are going to have to have some weird and maybe even tense conversations. So, we ask God to fill our mouths with His words. He is ready to do so. Maybe He is just waiting for us to ask.

Once we take a breath and pray, we move to the next step toward influence: we push through the fear.

Step #2 - Push Through the Fear

Here was Nehemiah, sad but wanting to influence. The king recognized his sadness and asked him about it. Nehemiah told him the reasons he was sad (Jerusalem was a mess). The king asked Nehemiah what he wanted. Nehemiah took a breath, said a quick prayer, and pushed through fear.

"I was very much afraid, but I said to the king, 'May the king live forever! Why should my face not look sad when the city where my ancestors are buried lies in ruins, and its gates have been destroyed by fire?'"
(Nehemiah 2:2-3; emphasis mine)

Nehemiah didn't say that he was afraid, he said that he was *very much* afraid. Why was he so scared? Because he was talking to the king! Our journey from sadness to influence will involve fearful conversations. Have them anyway. Your mouth will get dry. Your palms will sweat. Your heart will race. Push through the fear. Otherwise, you will stay stuck in sadness.

> **Push through the fear. Otherwise, you will stay stuck in sadness.**

Many times (if not most times), God will call you to something big, so huge that you are unable to do it without the help of others. Like Nehemiah, you may need to search out people with resources, connections, or money. You could easily let these folks intimidate. But you are on a mission. God has called you from sadness to influence, so pray and push in. You never know what is on the other side.

I fully understand the fear. A couple of years after my life changing phone call with a girl named Stephanie, I was experiencing another sadness: I was sad at the thought of not spending my life with her. I was crazy about this girl, and I felt the time was right for our relationship to go from dating to engaged. Before I proposed, I needed to influence her mother to give me her approval.

Saddened at the prospect of life without Steph, I made the decision to talk to her mother and ask for her blessing. My bones were filled with fear. But one night, I rallied all of the courage I could find. I picked up the phone and dialed her number. On the other end of the line, I heard her mom pick up.

"Hello."

I felt the blood drain from my head.

George Addar says, "Everything you want is on the other side of fear."[9] Fear is a crippler of influence. Push past it. Plow

> George Addar says, "Everything you want is on the other side of fear."

93

into it. Run over it. What lies on the other side is much better than where you are now.

At this point, you may wonder why fear is even part of the equation. If God really wants us to influence, couldn't He make it easier? Sure He could, but God often calls us to things that are much bigger than ourselves. I mean, if we could handle it on our own, we would do it without God. Funny thing is, He wants to do it *with* us. He will call us to change something we cannot do on our own, and when fear comes, He wants to use that as a trigger to lean on Him. He is brilliant like that.

> **If you want to fight greed, give something away.**

Our next step is closely tied to fear. After we have prayed and pushed through fear, it's time to ask.

Step #3: Ask

The king looked at Nehemiah and asked him what he wanted. Nehemiah was quick to respond:

"and I answered the king, 'If it pleases the king and if your servant has found favour in his sight, let him send me to the city in Judah where my ancestors are buried so that I can rebuild it.'

I also said to him, 'If it pleases the king, may I have letters to the governors of Trans-Euphrates, so that they will provide me safe-conduct until I arrive in Judah? And *may I have* a letter to Asaph, keeper of the royal park, so he will give me timber to make beams for the gates of the citadel by the temple and for the city wall and for the residence I will occupy?' And because the gracious hand of my God was on me, the king granted my requests" (Nehemiah 2:5-8; emphasis mine).

Nehemiah looked at the King and said, "I need some time off, and I need you to write letters to some of your boys to ask them to support my cause." This was no small ask. And yet here was Nehemiah. A moment earlier he was making sure the king's wine was good. Now he is making a huge request.

Nehemiah knew that to make the changes necessary in Jerusalem, he had to ask for resources from multiple places and direct them to one cause. Good influencers realize that this is the key to change. They take resources from different avenues and direct them to one source. But it all starts with the ask. If we don't make the ask, how can we expect to get what we need?

Loosen up the jaw. Rehearse the speech. Make the ask.

My jaw got pretty locked up when I was asking Stephanie's mom for her blessing. Last I left you with the story, her mom had just picked up the phone. She had no idea that I was about to ask for her daughter's hand in marriage.

I prayed and I pushed through fear. Then I asked the question.

"Terrie. This is Scot. I love your daughter and would like to ask her to marry me."

Silence. More silence. Followed by . . . silence.

"Well," came the response, slow and calm. "I suppose Dan and I will have to talk about that and get back with you."

"Thank you. Goodbye."

I felt sick, but I had pushed through the fear. I made the ask. Now I waited.

Just so I don't leave you hanging, a week after that phone call her mom did offer her approval and blessing. I know she took a huge risk on me, and I am grateful that she did.

At some point in the journey from sadness to influence, you will have to make an ask. Maybe you will ask . . .

"Will you marry me?"

"What do you think about me going back to college?"

"What do you think about us tithing?"

"Can we have coffee and talk about our friendship?"

"May I take you to dinner?"

"Would you be willing to invest money in this ministry?"

Make the ask. Dive into the awkward conversations. What's the worst that could happen?

Once we have made the ask, we move to our next and final step. It's time to act. Wait, what? I thought the asking was the act. Oh no, my friend. The world is influenced less by conversation and more by action.

Step #4: Act

Fresh from his conversation with the king, Nehemiah did not return to work, He kicked into action.

> "*I went* to Jerusalem, and after staying
> there three days *I set out* during
> the night with a few others. . . ."
> (Nehemiah 2:11-12 ; emphasis mine).

If we read on in Nehemiah 2, we read words like "went out" (Neh 2:13), "moved on," (Neh 2:14), "went up" (Neh 2:15), "turned back" (Neh 2:15), and "re-entered" (Neh 2:15). Nehemiah was on the move. He knew that it is impossible to influence without acting. If the situation is going to change, it will require us to act.

Action is risky. It takes putting ourselves out there. It makes us vulnerable. We may be hurt.

Action is risky.

We take action anyway. We may be misunderstood. We take action anyway. We may fail. We take action anyway.

Because we have been stung by disappointment, we tend to draw back and not make big moves. But big changes come from big moves.

As a side effect, your big moves encourage other people to make their own big moves. Those who are stuck in sadness see you becoming an influencer. They observe the change you instigate and figure, "If he can do it, maybe I can too." Your actions may be the courage others need.

Pray hard, push through fear, make big asks, and take action. Do. Not. Stop. The enemy wants us to wallow in our sadness. Our Father wants to use it for good. Redeem sadness by becoming an influential agent of change. Let's go!

> **Your actions may be the courage others need.**

A FINAL NOTE ON MOVING FROM SADNESS TO INFLUENCING CHANGE

Many times, our sadness is due to strained relationships with people: our kids, our exes, our parents, our in-laws, or our coworkers. As we move away from sadness, we will do our best to influence the relationships in hopes of making them better. Sometimes influence will work, sometimes it will not. When it comes to relationships, the other party must be open to change. I talk to people all the time who tell me about their strained relationships. They try to influence the relationship and make it better, but the other party wants little to do with change. I offer them the same advice the Apostle Paul offers:

> "If it is possible, *as far as it depends on you*, live at peace with everyone" (Romans 12:18; emphasis mine).

If you work your best to restore a relationship, and it does not end the way you desire, take comfort in knowing that you have done everything you can.

5

DITCH the Guilt

Determine the Emotion

Several years ago, I found myself in an upscale restaurant. I was invited to spend the evening sharing a gourmet meal with pastors of some of the largest churches in the US. Nothing was on the agenda except some conversation and steak (medium rare, please). I looked around the table in awe. These were some of the greatest church leaders in the country. I'm not sure how I got an invitation to the table, but I was happy to enjoy the food and the conversation. That is, until it got weird.

One of the pastors started talking about eschatology. Eschatology is the study of the end time, and there are several ideas on how exactly the end of the world will come. Every good pastor knows at least the major theories of eschatology, as well as the one he thinks holds the most truth. The conversation gained traction as most pastors shared their views. They talked about books, theories, and theological constructs. I could feel my heart start to race. I knew about end times. I studied it in school, but sitting around the table of pastors, I couldn't tell you the difference between any of the theories, let alone which one I thought was right.

This conversation was way over my head, and if this group knew that I knew nothing, they would think I was an imposter with no business being around the table. Given my track record of saying stupid things, I figured it best to keep my mouth shut and stay out of the conversation. I put my head down, focused on my steak and pretended not to hear the conversation. Then came the dagger.

"Scot, what eschatological view do you hold?"

Dramatic pause. Sickening feeling in my stomach.

Why does it seem like everyone at the table is staring at me? Is the room spinning? Jesus, I'm not sure of my view of the end times, but, if it is soon, like right now - this moment - this would be a great time for You to come back.

"Um, I'm sorry, what?" As if more time was going to help me.

"End times. What view do you hold?"

"Well, I hold the same view as Charlie."

Nice play. Charlie was the most respected pastor at the table. Nobody would argue with the view that Charlie (and I) held. The conversation moved to another pastor. Crisis averted. Or not.

As soon as I went back to carving my steak, I sensed the Holy Spirit. He only said one word:

"Liar."

Guilt flooded through me. Here I was, a pastor, blatantly lying to a group of my peers. The knot in my stomach caused me to lose my appetite. Instead of enjoying the company of my peers, I just wanted to go back to the hotel. I was filled with guilt.

Back at the hotel, I confessed the sin and asked God to give me strength not to do it again. The emotion of guilt had taken me to repentance (which is the purpose of God-provoked guilt), but I still needed to find the stronghold behind the action that caused the guilt.

IDENTIFY THE STRONGHOLD

Guilt is sometimes legitimate: It comes because we have taken an action that we should not have taken. As part of our mistake, we are filled with remorse. Other times, guilt is illegitimate: We have a guilt that shows up when we have not done anything wrong. The enemy loves to use false guilt to mess us up. Satan is an accuser (Rev 12:10), and he will often wrongly accuse us in order to make us feel guilty. As we break down the feeling of guilt with the "Why?" questions, we will be able to determine if the accusation of guilt has any merit. Let's run with my (embarrassing) example of guilt.

> Satan is an accuser, and he will often wrongly accuse us in order to make us feel guilty.

Question: **Why** do I feel guilty?

Answer: I lied. Straight up lied to a group of pastors.

Question: **Why** did you lie?

Answer: I felt if I told the truth I would be embarrassed.

Question: **Why** would you be embarrassed?

Answer: Because my peers would think less of me.

Question: **Why** do you want them to think much of you?

Answer: Because I want them to approve of me.

Question: **Why** is approval important?

Answer: Because I want to "be somebody."

As you can see, we have identified the stronghold. In this situation, the stronghold is, "I am only 'somebody' if others approve of me."

TRUTH THE STRONGHOLD

With the stronghold identified, we now apply the truth of scripture. It is here that we search the Bible and find truth. In this case, the stronghold is that my value is found in what others think of me. In my life, it is interesting how much this stronghold attaches to multiple emotions. Maybe the same is true for you as well. Good news: Sometimes there is a common stronghold behind multiple emotions. If that is the case, t hen we can kill one stronghold and impact multiple emotions.

CAPTURE THOUGHTS

Once we put the smack down on the lies that trigger guilt, we expect the enemy to bring other thoughts back at us:

- "You are an embarrassment."
- "You are unlovable."
- "You are a fake."

We capture those thoughts by thinking about what we are thinking about. We grab them and hold on to them.

When it comes to guilt, the enemy will sometimes lob doubt toward us:

- "Do you really think God forgave you?"
- "Do you really think He wants to use you since you embarrassed Him?"

Many of these thoughts will be seeds of doubt that question our forgiveness. We capture those thoughts, sprinkle some more truth on them if needed, and hand them over.

HAND IT TO JESUS

With our captured thought in hand, we give it to Jesus. This may be as simple as a prayer, or as aggressive as writing our angry thoughts and putting them in the God box (see chapter 1).

As God does, He uses all things together for good (Romans 8:28). He often uses guilt to deliver us from what is tripping us up.

FROM GUILT TO DELIVERANCE

Toasty was Grandma Grace's chihuahua. Were he alive today, I would have called him "The Toast," "Sir Toastiness," "Little T," or maybe just "Toast." Anyway, Toasty was a spry little mutt. He would do the tricks typical of a canine: beg, fetch, stare at you and leave you wondering if he was about to rip out your larynx. On occasion, Toasty would catch something from the corner of his eye, an object that always seemed to elude him. He would stop. Calming himself, he would summon his inner aggression. He sensed an enemy just behind him, and was ready to strike with vengeance.

> He sensed an enemy just behind him, and was ready to strike with vengeance.

From my vantage point, I always enjoyed watching this part of the show. Toasty was ready to attack . . . his tail. At a precise moment, he would bare his teeth and launch toward the pointy intruder. Funny thing: As he hurled toward the object of his wrath, the object moved as well (because it is connected to your rump, genius). The Toast (that's his new name, absolutely, I have decided) spun in constant circles. If I close my eyes, I can still hear his feet digging into Grandma's high-pile green shag carpet. The Toast was on a mission. Round and round he went, accomplishing absolutely nothing.

I have wondered how many miles Sir Toastiness (yea, I changed his name again) had spun on the shag. I wonder, if you took all the circles and straightened them into a line, where might this dog have traveled? Across the city? Halfway across the continent? Maybe to Alaska and back (breaking the heart of a cute husky along the way)? As it were, the mutt spun in circles, completely unproductive.

My biggest regrets in life are the seasons I spend chasing my tail. I want my spiritual life to take a straight line to Jesus, but instead I just run around in circles. Typically, my circle looks like this: I have my gaze on Jesus, but then I catch something out of the corner of my eye. It's sin, but it looks good, so I chase it. Unlike the pooch, I grab it. And I sin. And it feels great, for a moment. After I sin, I feel guilt. A terrible, gut-wrenching, "I'm-never-going-to-do-that-again" guilt. So, I repent (I tell God that I am sorry and that I will never do it again). When I repent, God forgives and delivers me. Then, He gives me peace. All is good. Except that I again see something out of the corner of my eye, and the whole process starts over again. Sin - Guilt - Repentance - Forgiveness - Peace. Like a dog chasing its tail, I get nowhere. Round and round, I am caught in this cycle.

Would your life be described as a straight line or a circle? What if you could be free from the sin that always seems to entice you? What if you could bust out of the circle?

The Lord does an interesting work to move us out of the circle. He uses guilt. Imagine what it would be like to catch a glimpse of sin out of the corner of your eye and, instead of chasing it, you walk away? Can you imagine a freedom like that? Freedom from the circle is possible. Are you tired of the guilt? Are you ready for some forgiveness and deliverance? If you are sick of running in a circle and ready to break out, let's go.

In Judges 3, we drop into a story about the people of Israel. Joshua led them into the promised land. God blessed them, and everything was looking up. Then Joshua died, and Israel went off the rails. They caught sight of sin, and, like a dog, they started the circle. Sin - Guilt - Repentance - Forgiveness - Peace. Repeated. Repeated again. Repeated some more.

In the middle of the chaos, God used a guy named Ehud. Ehud had one job, described to us in Judges 3.

> Again the Israelites cried out to the Lord,
> and he gave them a *deliverer*—
> Ehud, a left-handed man, the son
> of Gera the Benjamite. . . .
> (Judges 3:15; emphasis mine).

Here was Israel, under the weight of guilt, crying out to the Lord. (Can you relate?). Ehud came on scene and showed them how to get deliverance. When we talk about being delivered, we are not only talking about being delivered from our sins, we are talking about being delivered out of the circle of guilt.

In order to be delivered from the circle, we need to take some specific steps. We cannot "hope" our way out of the circle. The pull of sin is strong. Breaking its power will take determination and a series of specific steps. Let's look at the steps Ehud took in order to break Israel out.

> ## We cannot "hope" our way out of the circle.

Step 1: Determine what you are attacking

Ultimately, we are fighting Satan, but sometimes there is another foe that also needs attacked. Ehud got specific and targeted the enemy that was in sight.

> "... Eglon came and attacked Israel, and they took possession of the City of Palms. The Israelites were *subject to Eglon* king of Moab for eighteen years" (Judges 3:13-14; emphasis mine).

The word "subject" here means to be owned or controlled by something else. In this case, Israel was controlled by King Eglon. He was the enemy that needed to be attacked.

What is controlling you? Maybe it is selfishness, lust, acceptance, addiction, possessions, greed, or a hundred other masters. To determine what is controlling us, we look at the stronghold connected to our guilt. For example, we may feel guilty because we lied. Once we break that down and find the stronghold, we may realize that we have a stronghold of pride. Pride then becomes the focus of our attack. If we don't know what we are attacking, how are we going to get out of the circle?

Over the years at our church, we have hired several people. It is no easy task to get on staff with us. Applicants must produce resumes, references, and videos. They undergo an extensive background check. They spend the weekend with us and go through upwards of eight interviews. Depending on the position we are hiring, sometimes I do a one-on-one interview with a candidate. I only ask two questions, but they may be the most challenging of the interviews.

Typically, I will pick a candidate up at his hotel. For the next 30 minutes, I have him trapped in the car. (He could escape, but it's not going to be easy.) I warm him up by telling him that the answers to these questions are confidential. I also inform him that these may be the most pointed questions he is asked. Usually I get a timid, "Ohhhhkayy?" Sometimes I speed the car up and check that the doors are locked. Then, I drop the bomb.

> Sometimes I speed the car up and check that the doors are locked. Then, I drop the bomb.

> **Question 1:** "What will I learn about you in six months that will surprise or embarrass me?"

> **Question 2:** "If you were hired and then later had to resign from our church due to a moral failure, what would that moral failure be?"

This is usually followed by a period of silence.

I don't ask these questions in order to be mean. I'm not trying to prove a point. I don't intend to shame anyone. I simply want to know his weak points so that we know what we should be attacking. I want to help him in the fight, but

I can't help him attack if we don't know what we are battling.

How would you answer those questions? Once you answer them honestly, you will know what to fight. Otherwise, you are swinging at air.

Back to our boy, Ehud. Once he realized what he was attacking (King Eglon), he moved to the next step.

Step #2: Decide a plan of action

Once we determine what we are attacking, our temptation is to run and mow it down. Not so fast. Our enemy is crafty (Gen 3:1). He is no dummy. We need a plan if we are going to choke the life out of him. Ehud was aware that an attack needed to be well thought out. Our story continues . . .

> "Again the Israelites cried out to the Lord, and he gave them a deliverer—Ehud, a left-handed man, the son of Gera the Benjamite. *The Israelites sent him with tribute to Eglon king of Moab.* Now Ehud had made a double-edged sword about a cubit long, which he

116

strapped to his right thigh under
his clothing"
(Judges 3:15-16; emphasis mine).

Ehud identified King Eglon as the enemy. He must take him out. To do so, he crafted a clever plan. He went to the king with tribute (a gift). Ehud outsmarted King Eglon in two arenas: For one, he pretended to be an admirer of the king by bringing him a gift. Two, he had a sword on his right thigh.

The significance of having a sword on his right thigh is that it goes undetected. Those who served the king would pat down a visitor for weapons, but they would not likely check the right thigh. Most people are right-handed and would keep a sword on their left thigh, so that they could draw it quickly. Ehud, being a leftie, kept his sword on the right thigh. Brilliant plan, Ehud.

Ehud walked into the presence of his enemy armed with a sword. Much is the same today. When we fight against our enemy, we fight with a sword. Our sword is the truth of scripture (Eph 6:17). We then apply truth to our enemy. Our weapon is truth. Look at it like this:

Satan is called the "father of lies" (John 8:44). There is zero truth in him. When he tempts us to sin (and stay in the circle), lies surround the sin. Lies like:

- "This will be fine."
- "Everybody is doing it."
- "Just this one time."
- "Nobody will know."
- "It won't hurt anyone."

His chief strategy is to deny, confuse, misrepresent, or counterfeit whatever God has said. However, God's native language is truth. So, truth has to be part of our attack plan. This is exactly what Jesus is talking about when he says, "Sanctify them by the truth; your word is truth" (John 17:17).

Our source of truth is not in our own ideas or the advice of others. Our truth is found in the Bible. The most powerful plan of attack uses the sword: the truth of scripture.

It is interesting to note that Ehud (this guy is no joke) went on the offensive, not the defensive. He didn't wait for the king to come to him and attack. He had the audacity to walk into the presence of the king with the plan to take him out. It's like he woke up that morning, poured himself a bowl of Wheaties, cranked up "Eye of the Tiger," strapped on his sword, and made a straight line to the palace. He woke up ready to pick a fight.

We should do the same. How about we stop playing defense? How about we make a new plan: As soon as we wake up, we look for a fight. Let's stop waiting for the stronghold to come to us. Let's go wake it up and beat it down with truth. I imagine it could look like this:

We wake up in the morning, and before any other thought can jump in our minds, we read Romans 8 out loud.

> "And if the Spirit of him who raised Jesus from the dead is living in you, he who raised Christ from the dead will also give life to your mortal bodies because of his Spirit who lives in you" (Romans 8:11).

Now that we have the sword (truth) in hand, we are ready to fight, so we address our foe.

> "Good morning addiction. Before you make a play, I would like to remind you that the same power that raised Christ

from the dead is at work in me, so unless
you are feeling like a beat-down today,
don't mess with me."

How about this one?

"See what great love the Father has
lavished on us, that we should be called
children of God! And that is what we are!"
(1 John 3:1)

With that truth in hand, our plan is to wake up
any negative thoughts.

"Good morning, negative thoughts.
Before you try to convince me that I am
lonely and abandoned, I want to remind
you of some truth - God is my Father and
I am His child. Unless your father is more
powerful than mine, you might want to
step away. I'm pretty sure my Daddy
can beat up yours."

Or this:

"For we know that our old self was
crucified with him so that the body ruled
by sin might be done away with, that we

should no longer be slaves to sin—because anyone who has died has been set free from sin" (Romans 6:6-7).

"Hey anger - you up yet? Let me wake you with this truth - I will not serve you today, or any day for that matter. You have no hold on me. I am not your slave. I found a better Master. Find someone else. I have more important things to do for my Master today."

One more?

"For God has not given us a spirit of fear, but of power and of love and of a sound mind" (2 Timothy 1:7; NKJ).

"Hey, fear, wake up! You are probably plotting against me today. I just wanted you to know that I only take what my Father gives me. He gives me power, love, and a sound mind. I'm not making room for anything in my life that is not from God. And last I checked; He doesn't give out fear. Find somewhere else to go. You are not welcome or invited here."

Whew! That fires me up! Go on the offensive my friends. Let your guilt lead you to deliverance! Identify the enemy and make a plan. While you do, don't forget about the third step we learn from Ehud.

Step #3: Don't feed your enemy

What do we know about the enemy, King Eglon? We know he is a king. We know he has power. We know he has several followers. I picture him maybe mid 30's, tall, thick. Long black hair. Perhaps a battle scar or two on well-chiseled skin. Maybe he looked like Gaston (you know, from *Beauty and the Beast*). Could be that he wakes up every morning in his antler-decorated house, downs 5 dozen eggs and admires himself in the mirror. You get the picture. King Eglon is likely an enemy of stature. Powerful. Strong. Here is how the Bible describes him:

> "He presented the tribute to Eglon king of
> Moab, who was a very fat man"
> (Judges 3:17).

Big bad King Eglon is a fat man. Very fat, actually. The guy bringing all this oppression is nothing but an out of shape fellow pretending to be powerful, just like our enemy. It's all smoke and mirrors, friend. While our enemy is crafty, he is less powerful than our Father. As a matter of fact, he is less powerful than the Holy Spirit who lives inside of us (Romans 8:11).

Who gave King Eglon power? The people under him. Who fattens up King Eglon? The people under him. Who fattens up our enemies? Sometimes, we do. My friend, stop feeding what is trying to kill you.

> ## Stop feeding what is trying to kill you.

"Man, I need some help, with a, well, you know . . . ." A guy came up to me at church, wanting some help in leaving a sinful circle.

"Yes?" I answered.

"Well, you know man, I just need to stop looking at porn, and so I could use some accountability."

"Fair enough," was my reply. "Here is what we will do. We will install some software on your phone and computer. When you slip up and look at porn, you and I are going to go and talk to your wife and tell her what you have done."

He paused. "Oh, hey, man. No. Like, um, I just need someone to, you know, help me not do it. I mean, it's not that big of an issue."

End of conversation.

Let me write the next chapter in that guy's story: He will *wish* that he would stop looking at porn. He will *hope* that he won't look at porn, but he really doesn't want to kill it. Part of him still wants to keep it around just in case he ever wants to run back to it. His pornography addiction will not stop. He will live life chasing his tail. He will roll through Sin – Guilt – Repentance – Forgiveness – Peace a thousand times. You cannot get out of the circle and find deliverance if you still feed the enemy. Whatever you feed gets fat. And powerful. And hangs around. Don't think for a minute that this is some kind of game.

Several years ago, we took in a rescue dog. She was a cute pup we named *Nestle* (as in the makers of delicious candy and snacks). Nestle was fun and energetic. Funny thing is, she kept hanging around – mostly because we fed her. No worries, Nestle was an innocent, friendly dog, or so we thought. Nestle, we discovered, was a biter. Not a nibbler, not a growler, but a biter.

She would not tear your limb off, but she would also not leave you with a nibble. On more than one occasion she drew blood, not to the point of stitches, but enough that you knew she meant business. Anytime someone came through our front door we immediately yelled, "Do not touch the dog!" This usually confused our guests for one simple reason; Nestle was so darn cute.

If you came to our home, Nestle would run up to you as if to say, "Hi." Her tail would wag in excitement. You would look at her beautiful brown eyes and bend down as you say, "What a cute little puppy." As soon as your hand touched her head, out came the teeth to meet your flesh. Every time.

That's exactly how it is with the sin that catches our eyes. It runs up to us; it looks good. It begs us to engage. And when we do, we get bit. Every time.

> We cannot feed sin without getting bit.

To have hope of deliverance, we have to stop feeding the sin. Cut off the supply. Stop keeping it close. Don't throw it any crumbs. We cannot feed sin without getting bit. It's time to starve it out so that we can walk out of the circle.

At this point, like Ehud, we have determined what we are attacking, we have decided a plan of action, and we have stopped feeding the enemy. It is here that the story of Ehud takes an interesting turn. In the king's presence, with a plan in place, and a sword on his thigh, you would think Ehud would do what he comes to do. Instead, he walks out. Wait, What? Yep. Which brings us to our next step and some encouragement:

Step #4: Don't chicken out

For whatever reason, Ehud walked out of the king's presence. It appears that the circle will continue. There would be no deliverance. The plan was in place. The enemy was in sight. Instead of killing the king, Ehud gave him a gift and then made an exit. Talk about feeding the enemy. However, that is all about to change. We pick up the story as Ehud walked away.

"But on reaching the stone images near Gilgal *he himself went back to Eglon* and said, 'Your Majesty, I have a secret message for you.' The king said to his attendants, 'Leave us!' And they all left (Judges 3:19; emphasis mine).

Ehud stopped. He pondered. He turned around and headed back to the king. Something caused him to rethink the plan, but what? The clue is found in the beginning of verse 9. Ehud saw the stone images. Looking at the images gave him the courage to turn around and finish the job. What in the world do statues have to do with all of this? As it turns out, everything.

When Ehud looked at the images, he realized that they were images to a god other than the God of Israel. He was reminded that there was a battle going on, and the fight was for the supremacy of his God. He was reminded of his mission to bring freedom and to get all of Israel out of the circle. Walking away from the king, Ehud might think, "This king *should* die." Once he saw the images, he realized that the king *must* die.

Today, make the declaration that enough is enough. It's time to do something about the sin that has you in the circle. When it comes time, you will be tempted to chicken out. Do. Not. Walk. Away. Go back and do what you came to do. Reengage in the fight. It does not matter that you fell off the wagon or got drug into the circle of sin again. Get up and dust yourself off. Do. Not. Chicken. Out.

Finally, we get to the last step of our deliverance. Insert the dramatic movie score, it's all come down to this.

Step #5: Decimate (Take the kill shot)

We will never get out of the circle unless we take the kill shot. It's not enough to hope it all gets better. The sin in your life must die. Since it has made its way into your life, it is trespassing. In this case trespassers don't get asked to l eave. They don't even get a letter of eviction. They get shot.

Back to the dramatic ending of the very fat king:

"But on reaching the stone images near Gilgal he himself went back to Eglon and said, 'Your Majesty, I have a secret message for you.' The king said to his attendants, 'Leave us!' And they all left. Ehud then approached him while he was sitting alone in the upper room of his palace and said, 'I have a message from God for you.' As the king rose from his seat, Ehud reached with his left hand, drew the sword from his right thigh and plunged it into the king's belly. Even the handle sank in after the blade, and his bowels discharged. Ehud did not pull the sword out, and the fat closed in over it" (Judges 3:20-22).

This reads like a movie script. Ehud came in all like,"I have a secret message for you." Fat king thought, "Awesome, secrets for me, the king." That was the moment we have been waiting for. Ehud grabbed the concealed sword and killed the king. I do wonder if, as he sank in the blade, Ehud whispered in the king's ear, "The secret message my king is this: My name is Inigo Montoya. You killed my Father! Prepare to die!"

Okay, maybe not, but none-the-less, what a great example we get from Ehud. By killing the enemy, he brings deliverance to Israel. It would not be enough to wound the enemy. He had to die. Friend, if you want out of the circle, your sin must die. Kill the porn. Go to the AA meeting. Make the call. Flush the pills. End the relationship. Do what you have to do. Do not walk away. Do not back down. Life is at stake.

Because God uses all things for good, He will sometimes use guilt to bring us to deliverance. In doing so, follow the same steps that we learn from Ehud:

Step #1: Determine what you are attacking.

Step #2: Decide a plan of action.

Step #3: Don't feed your enemy.

Step #4: Don't chicken out.

Step #5: Decimate. Take the kill shot.

SOME FINAL THOUGHTS

Can you imagine what life is like outside of the circle? Can you imagine sin not having a hold on you? Imagine seeing a temptation out of the corner of your eye, and instead of turning *toward* it, you turn *away* from it. You can do it. I have walked out of the circle. I have seen friends walk out of the circle. You have everything you need. Freedom is close.

May the Holy Spirit-induced guilt drive you to deliverance and freedom. May you never forget that you are a warrior. I'll leave you with these reminders:

"For everyone born of God overcomes the world. This is the victory that has overcome the world, even our faith. Who is it that overcomes the world?

Only the one who believes that Jesus is the Son of God" (1 John 5:4-5).

"But the Lord is with me like a mighty warrior; so my persecutors will stumble and not prevail.

They will fail and be thoroughly disgraced; their dishonor will never be forgotten" (Jeremiah 20:11).

6

DITCH the Fear & Anxiety

DETERMINE THE EMOTION

I'm not sure when anxiety entered my life, but I know it was at a young age. It was not birthed in some traumatic event. At some point, worry took root and it began to grow. It would manifest itself in me closing my eyes tightly when I blinked or shaking my head in short twitches. I would worry most of the time about almost everything. While not constant, it was annoying. As a kid, my parents had noticed the anxiety in me. They sought treatment with both psychologists and medical doctors. No real solution was found, so I just continued on.

By the time I was in middle school, the anxiety was at an all-time high. This season is typically rough for most students, but for me, it was crushing. My greatest nemesis was the school bus.

> My greatest nemesis was the school bus.

Every morning, I would stand at the bus stop and wait for the bus. I was one of the last stops on the route. By the time the bus got to me, it was full, every seat taken. In order to find a place to sit, I would have to ask someone to scoot over and shove three people in an already crowded seat. Nobody ever offered me a seat. They either shook their head "no" or rolled their eyes as if to say, "You are a moron. I don't want you to sit in my seat. I do not like you. At all."

To add to the traveling tube of stress and hatred, the bus was full of middle school and high school students. As a young middle schooler, I was at the bottom of the food chain.

The riding of the bus produced so much stress and anxiety in me that I made an alternate plan; I would ride my bike to and from school. Every morning, I would leave my house and ride three and a half miles to school. In the evening, I would make the return trip home. Seven miles round trip is a long commute, but I was motivated to do whatever I could to escape the anxiety.

The problem with my escape plan was that I was not escaping the anxiety. I was not killing it; I was running from it. It would eventually come around again. As the Indiana weather turned cold, I realized I was in trouble. A kid can't ride seven miles in the pouring rain, sleet, or snow. I would eventually have to face the bus of fear. =

What is your "bus"? What has you plagued with fear and anxiety? Whatever it is, don't jump on a bike and ride away from fear. Run toward it. The Lord knows that we will deal with fear. Do you know what the most repeated command of the Bible is? "Do not fear." Over 365 times in the Bible God encourages His followers not to fear. 365! That's one for each day of the year.

So, my anxious friends, let's get a hold on this. Let's break it down so that we can find some freedom and put fear and anxiety behind us.

IDENTIFY THE STRONGHOLD

When fear or worry come to mind, we stop and think about what we are thinking about. Instead of our worry running us, we stop and dissect the worry.

As we break down the feeling of worry with the "Why?" questions, the stronghold will be revealed. For this example, let's use social anxiety. Many of us are introverted. The thought of meeting new people is sometimes uncomfortable and paralyzing. Let's say that you are about to start a new job. Or a new semester at school. Or you are joining a new small group. Or you are working with a new team at work. Whatever the situation, you feel the worry and anxiety rising inside of you. Let's ask the "Why?" questions and get to the stronghold.

Question: **Why** do I feel anxiety?

Answer: I am going to a place where I don't know people.

Question: **Why** does it bother you that you don't know people?

Answer: They may ignore me and not talk to me.

Question: **Why** would that bother you?

Answer: It would make me feel like an outcast. I would feel unloved and unwanted.

Question: Do you often feel you are unloved and unwanted?

Answer: Yes, I am unloved and unwanted.

STOP! Sometimes the "Why?" questions will lead to a deep revelation. In this case, we may not want to go to a place where we meet new people because they could make us feel unloved and unwanted. The reason this comes to the surface is because we are already feeling unloved and unwanted. This is a positive revelation because it allows us to identify the stronghold. In this case, the stronghold is a feeling of being unloved or unwanted. That feeling was already there; the situation just served to expose it. Now that we know the stronghold, we can start to dismantle it.

TRUTH THE STRONGHOLD

Once we find the stronghold, we apply the truth of scripture to it. It is here that we search the Bible and find truth. In this case, the stronghold is that we feel unaccepted and unloved. (We will put a huge truth beat down on this stronghold later in the chapter.)

CAPTURE THOUGHTS

Once we truth the stronghold, the enemy will come back with thought grenades. His hope is to allow those toxic thoughts to be planted where they can re-establish the strongholds in our lives. What he does not realize is that we are much smarter and much more powerful than he is.

When the fearful and anxious thoughts come, we capture them by thinking about what we are thinking about. We grab them and hold onto them.

When it comes to worry, the enemy will sometimes lob doubt towards us.

- "They won't like you."
- "You will be ignored."
- "Nobody wants you or needs you."
- "You are not worth loving."

When those thoughts come, we capture them, sprinkle some more truth on them if needed, and hand them over.

HAND IT TO JESUS

With our captured thoughts in hand, we give them to Jesus. This may be as simple as a prayer or as aggressive as writing out what makes us anxious thoughts ("Jesus, I am worried about . . .") and putting them in the God box (see chapter 1)

FROM FEAR TO IDENTITY

I'm astounded by how many of my actions are based in fear. I watch what I eat because I fear I will gain weight. I watch my words because I fear I will say something stupid. I fear spending money because I may go broke. I fear failing, so I don't take a risk. Slowly, over time, I chain myself to fear. I constantly ask myself, "Scot, what are you afraid of?"

> I'm astounded by how many of my actions are based in fear.

What about you? What are you afraid of? What brings anxiety into your life? Maybe you fear your car may break down and leave you with a large repair bill. Maybe you are afraid of getting married, or not getting married. Maybe anxiety has crept in because you are not dating. Or, maybe you are dating, and it is not going well. Maybe you have a fear of asking her out. Maybe you worry about health issues, grades, relationships, or a thousand other situations. Maybe, like me, some days you worry about everything.

What if we could shake off worry? What if we could live without anxiety? What if fear could fade? Friend, it is possible. The journey from fear to freedom comes when we remind ourselves of who we are.

Let me say that again so we catch it: The journey from fear to freedom comes when we remind ourselves of who we are.

The truth of who we are is found in scripture. Let's take a deep dive into scripture and allow it to inform us of who we really are. The more we know the Bible, the more we know the truth of who we are.

I love what my friend Dick Eastman says about fear and the Bible:

> "There are only three classes of people
> in the world today a preacher confessed.
> Those who are afraid, those who
> don't know enough to be afraid, and
> those who know their Bibles."
> (*The Hour that Changes the World*.
> Dick Eastman. 33-34)[10]

In the book of Luke, Jesus directly addresses fear. It's as if He knew that we would deal with fear on the daily.

"I tell you, my friends, do not be afraid of those who kill the body and after that can do no more. But I will show you whom you should fear: Fear him who, after your body has been killed, has authority to throw you into hell. Yes, I tell you, fear him. Are not five sparrows sold for two pennies? Yet not one of them is forgotten by God. Indeed, the very hairs of your head are all numbered. Don't be afraid; you are worth more than many sparrows (Lk 12:4-7).

Tucked away in Luke 12, we find some truth that takes us from fear to freedom. Buckle up, this is going to be a fun ride.

FROM FEAR TO IDENTITY
SHUT DOWN YOUR FEAR WITH THESE TRUTHS:

Truth #1: You are remembered

"Are not five sparrows sold for two pennies? Yet *not one of them is forgotten by God...*" (Luke 12:6; emphasis mine).

As a young family, we frequented the local building supply store. (Again, a 100-year-old house meant that we were constantly in reconstruction mode.) One particular day Steph and I took our two daughters to the store. We made our way to the flooring section. While there, we engaged in a lengthy conversation with an employee. We were determining the best materials, installation, and price for a project. I'm not sure how long we were there, but somewhere in the middle of the conversation, we heard a voice on the loudspeaker: "We have a lost little girl at customer service. She is looking for her mommy and daddy. Please come to customer service to claim her."

I stopped our conversation and turned around so that I could take a quick inventory of my two kids and get back to business. "One . . . one. Um, Mariah, where is your sister?"

We made our way to customer service. There was found Maddy. She was understandably shaken.

> "Dad," she said, "You forgot me.

"Dad," she said, "You forgot me. You forgot me!"

"Baby," I assured her, "I did not forget you. I could never forget you. And let's be clear;

you wandered off from me. I did not wander off from you."

When we experience fear, it is often because we feel like we are forgotten. "If you remembered me, God, all of this chaos would not be happening. I would not be in the middle of sickness, or divorce, or a strained relationship or job struggles, or . . . ." He has not forgotten you; He has not left you. He has not wandered off. Just because the circumstances are crazy does not mean that He has checked out.

This idea of feeling like God has left us is nothing new. In the book of Isaiah, we eavesdrop on a conversation about feeling forgotten:

"But Zion said, "The Lord has forsaken me, the Lord has forgotten me." 'Can a mother forget the baby at her breast and have no compassion on the child she has borne?

Though she may forget, I will not forget you! See, I have engraved you on the palms of my hands; your walls are ever before me'" (Isaiah 49:14–16).

God's people (like my Maddy) were saying, "You have forgotten us!" God's response? "It is impossible for Me to forget you. Mothers don't forget their babies, and I don't forget you." As if to add to His case, God makes a fascinating statement about engraving. He says, "See, I have engraved you on the palms of my hands (Is 49:16).

We believe God was referring to a practice of engraving. This practice included taking a hot item (like a hot iron from a fire) and burning it into the skin. The burned skin would then be rubbed with henna, indigo, or another colored substance. Think of it like an ancient tattoo. Here it is as if God is saying, "I have tattooed you on my hand as a permanent reminder. I will never forget you."

I am also fascinated by the reference to the engraving of a hand. When Christ was crucified on the cross, they are said to have driven spikes through His wrists (the area of the hand). It is as if God is also saying, "Look at the scars from the nails. These are a reminder that you are remembered. The scars remind Me of you."

Friend, you are remembered. He has not forgotten about you. He has not dumped you. He has not left you. He loves you more than you know. Don't let the circumstances lie to you. He has not checked out. He has not run away. He remembers you.

> ## He has not dumped you.

Not only does the Bible teach us that we are remembered, but it offers another truth.

Truth #2: You are known

> "Indeed, the very *hairs of your head are all numbered.* Don't be afraid; you are worth more than many sparrows"
> (Luke 12:7; emphasis mine).

"The red-headed brothers." Often my brother, Darel, and I would be referred to as such. We both had red hair and similar facial features. We grew up only two years apart. In most cases we experienced life together as if we were twins. We would ride bikes together, fight, build forts, have adventures, and we even played music together in a few bands (I'm certain you heard of us. We were kind of a big deal in the music scene. At least according to Mom and Dad.)

While Darel and I are not twins, together we shared experiences: the same biological parents, the same way of thinking, and many of the same friends. Darel knows me and I know him. I know how he thinks, and he knows how I think. I know what he would do in a situation, and he knows what I would do. I get him. He gets me.

As I write this, Darel, a full-bird colonel in the Air Force, is currently stationed in a hostile country in the Middle East. The last few days we have been communicating via text, sharing stories and concerns of life. We both know that we can't have conversations like this with just anyone. But there is something special about brothers; they are known by each other.

There is something better than being known by a brother; being known by our Creator. That's hard to get our heads around. The Creator of the universe, the One who set everything in motion, the One who parted the sea and raised the dead, He *knows* us. The fact that He knows us should melt some fear.

How well does He know us? According to Luke 12:7, He knows us so well that He knows the number of hairs on our head. (That's pretty easy for me: zero.) Think about the person you know best. Your BFF. The one who has confided in you. The one you have known for years. You know everything about him. The good and the bad. Since you know him so well, let me ask you a question: How many hairs does he have on his head?

When God states that He knows the number of hairs on our heads, it is possible that He is making some deeper statements. First, I believe He is saying that He knows us better than we know ourselves. He not only knows our follicle count, He knows our chemical makeup, our past, our future, our doubts, our fears, our regrets, our subconscious. We are deeply and intimately known by Him. I don't know about you, but just knowing that I am known by Him causes my fear to start fading.

Secondly, (and I find this astounding), I believe God is stating that He *constantly* knows us, even as we are changing. Follow me on this. The inventory on your head is changing every day. Average hair loss is around 100 strands per day.[11] When God says that He knows the number of hairs on your head, He didn't just take inventory last year and called it good. He knows your number every day. He is a God that knows us even as we are changing. He knows the changing situations, the changing moods, the changing challenges, and the changing joys. He is with us constantly in the change, and we are known even as everything around us changes.

Not only are we are constantly known, but we are also *deeply* known. Jesus reminds us of this when He says

> "I am the good shepherd; *I know my sheep* and my sheep know me— *just as the Father knows me and I know the Father*—and I lay down my life for the sheep" (John 10:14-15; emphasis mine).

Jesus also reminds us that not only is He a shepherd, He is a friend. In Luke 12:14, He says, "I tell you, *my friends*, do not be afraid of those who kill the body and after that can do no more."

The Creator of the Universe has a name for you: "My friend." You probably know thousands of people. There are probably hundreds of people who know your name. Maybe some people would call you "a friend." Jesus, the crucified and risen Son of God, looks at you and says, "My friend."

You may think, "God doesn't call me His friend. I have done nothing to deserve His friendship." Correct! We are His friends, not because of what we have or have not done, but because of His love for us. My friend Michele Cushatt reminded me of this. In a recent book, Michele so eloquently states, "He meets us there. Not because we deserve it, but because His covenant love can't help it."[12]

You are a friend of God. You are known. And the one who knows you is much bigger than whatever is behind your fear.

Luke gives us another truth which will help shut down fear. Not only are you remembered, and known, but you are also valuable.

> You are a friend of God. You are known. And the one who knows you is much bigger than whatever is behind your fear.

Truth #3: You are valuable

"Indeed, the very hairs of your head
are all numbered. Don't be afraid; *you are
worth more than many sparrows*"
(Luke 12:7; emphasis mine).

In this verse, Jesus makes a connection between value and fear. Many times, we feel fear when we don't feel valuable. Because we don't feel valuable, we believe that we will not be protected.

As my daughters got older, they would encounter situations which caused fear. They might have been situations at school, work, or with friends. Many times they would come to me for advice. In almost every situation, I would say the same thing. "Listen to me carefully. I am your father. You are my daughter. You are not in this alone. I have resources and connections. I will do whatever I can to make sure that whatever you are facing does not take you down."

> Many times, we feel fear when we don't feel valuable.

Usually after those conversations, the fear would fade a notch or two. Just by being reminded that they are valued, my daughters gained more courage in the face of fear.

The devil will want to send a different message. He will try to convince you that you are not worth much to God. He will lay down some lies. Lies like . . .

- "You are not worth much anyway. Why would God watch over you?"

- "After all you have done, do you really think that God thinks much of you?"

- "If God thought you had any value at all, why would you even be in this mess in the first place?"

Lies. Lies. Lies. You have value because He created you. You have deep value because you said "yes" to Jesus and made Him the leader of your life. You have much more value than you realize. How much value? Glad you asked! In Matthew 13, Jesus makes a statement concerning our value.

"Again, the kingdom of heaven is like a merchant looking for fine pearls. When he found one of great value, he went away and sold everything he had and bought it" (Matthew 13:45-46).

For years, I looked at this scripture and missed what it was saying. In this passage, we have two main features: One, the merchant; and two, the pearl. We often interpret the scripture like this:

The merchant = you and I
The pearl = Jesus

The above idea makes sense. We (the merchants) look for Jesus (the pearl). When we find Him, we see that He is so valuable that we give up everything in order to find Him. While it is true that we give up our entire lives to follow Jesus, I am not convinced that this is what Jesus was teaching in this particular parable. I believe there is another way to look at this parable:

The merchant = Jesus
The pearl = you and I

How could I make such a conclusion? Look at the first part of the verse: "The kingdom of heaven is like . . ." When Jesus talks about the kingdom of heaven, He is talking about the way in which God operates. So, it is highly probable that Jesus is saying, "The way in which God operates is like a merchant . . ." Understanding that possible twist gives the parable an entirely new meaning. If Jesus is the merchant and you are the pearl of great price, He chased you. As a matter of fact, He went away and sold everything He had. That is, He gave up His life on a cross for you - because you have great value. Let that soak in. Do not dismiss the fact that you are of great value. Sure, you are not the center of the universe. You shouldn't walk around arrogantly, but you should walk around in the reality of this fact: You are of great value.

Can we go a little deeper in this whole idea of you having great value? The story of the gospel is that you and I sin. In God's economy, sins must be punished. However, God thinks you are so valuable that He makes a way for the punishment of your sin to be transferred to someone else. He allowed Christ to be crucified on a bloody cross. The punishment for our sins was put on Christ. If we choose to ask God to forgive us, the punishment for our sins is transferred to Christ.

The story of the cross is a story of how much God values us, but as we go deeper, it gets better. Think about it like this: God is all-sufficient. A simple way to say that He is all-sufficient is to say that He does not need anything or anyone in

> **The punishment for our sins was put on Christ.**

order to be "more" God. He already is all that He needs to be. No amount of people following Him is going to change who God is. In short, He does not need us in order to be God. So then, His motivation for allowing Christ to die a terrible death on the cross had nothing to do with Him. God would still be God if Jesus would not have died. Why then, did Jesus die?

For us.

For me.

For you.

The death, burial, and resurrection of Jesus is a declaration that God has found great value in those He created. Never, ever - EVER, forget that you are a pearl, a treasure of great price. Your Heavenly Father thinks that you have deep value. Have no fear, He watches over everything that He values.

A FINAL WORD: EITHER WAY, YOU WIN

When anxiety comes, I have asked myself, "What is the absolute worst thing that could happen?" After some thinking, I concluded that the worst thing that could happen is that I would die. For many, dying is the pinnacle of all fear.

What if we could face death without fear? If we could conquer the fear of dying, wouldn't that lower our anxiety for whatever tomorrow has in store for us?

Last year, I sat with my Uncle Jack. Instead of sharing a cup of coffee, we were lounging in hospital chairs as he took his weekly round of chemo. Diagnosed with cancer, Uncle Jack was filling his body with chemicals in the hope that the cancer would disappear. To be honest, it was a long shot. For the past couple of years, his body had been in a slow decay. Uncle Jack was facing death. He was staring fear straight in the eyes. This was no game. There was a high probability that the treatment would be unsuccessful. Death was a probability.

Sitting together in the hospital, we talked about life. He brought me up to date on his regimen. We dug up some old memories. We even chuckled. In the middle of a cancer ward, with the reality that life could soon end, we laughed. I prayed with Uncle Jack. I thanked God for him and again begged God to heal his body. When I finished praying, we both wiped some tears. As I was leaving, he stopped me. "Hey, Scot." I turned around and saw my frail Uncle Jack. He cracked a smile and gave me a thumbs up. He then spoke the last audible words I would hear from him:

"Either way, I win."

Either. Way. I. Win.

A few weeks later, Uncle Jack drew his last breath on earth and his first in heaven. He won. I am sure he had fear and anxiety as he faced death, but I am confident that he knew that he was remembered by God, he was known by God, and that he was valuable to God.

Whatever situation is causing anxiety, my deep hope is that you will know beyond a shadow of a doubt that you are remembered, known, and valued. I know the road is not easy. But I also know that our God is great. Let me pray for you.

God, thank You for my friends reading these words. Though we may not have met, I ask that You intersect their worries. I ask that You help them know that You have not forgotten them. Let Your Holy Spirit convince them that they are known. I ask that they physically feel that they are valuable. I thank You that my friends are not in the fight alone. Do Your work, God. Break the chains of anxiety. Bring freedom. And as You do, we declare Your greatness. When we tell our story of freedom, we will make You center stage as our Healer. We love You. We are confident that You love us. Thank You for Your presence and Your healing. In the powerful name of Jesus, we pray. Amen.

"The Lord is for me; I will not fear; What can man do to me?" (Psalm 118:6; NASB)

7

DITCH the Discouragement

DETERMINE THE EMOTION

3:00 a.m. I woke to the sound of dripping. The evening had brought a thunderstorm and heavy rain. This was typical for a midwestern summer night. Cracks of thunder, the rustle of leaves, and heavy wind were all familiar sounds. However, the constant drip — drip — drip was something new, and strangely loud.

I rose from bed and followed the sound. The volume increased as I walked into our dining room. *Drip-drip-DRIP,* the sound of water hitting a wood floor. I turned on the dining room light. My stomach dropped. Along the ceiling was a row of small water droplets, all poised to make their way from ceiling to floor. It took me all of two seconds to diagnose the situation. My roof was leaking, badly. I took a deep breath and tried not to panic. Somewhere in that moment, a seed of discouragement was planted.

I grabbed some large plastic totes and placed them under the drips. Since there was not much more I could do at that moment, I went back to bed for a sleepless night. The next morning I had collected around 15 gallons of water. The seed of discouragement was growing.

Being the kind of guy who tries to fix stuff on his own, I figured I would try to find the leak. Nice wish. As I walked on my roof the next day, I found nothing except a roof (I'm not exactly a trained roofer). My quick inspection told me the shingles were old. I was reminded of what the home inspector told us when we bought the house: "You are going to need a new roof very soon." That was five years earlier. I laid down a blue tarp over where I thought the leak was coming from and hoped for the best. The next night we had another storm with more rain on my roof and (you guessed it) more rain in my house. Discouraged again.

Realizing that we needed a new roof, I again decided that I could tackle the project. I would rally some friends and we would strip off the old roof and put on a new one. I mean, how hard could it be? Evidently, *very* hard. A new installation was way over my head. I would have to hire professionals. The discouragement was growing and about to get worse.

I don't know if you have ever collected estimates for a new roof. If you have not, prepare yourself for sticker shock. We were presented with quotes between $12,000 and $40,000. I could not believe the figures. I was not living in a castle. This was a small, older house. I didn't have $12,000 (let alone $40,000), and my roof was falling apart. I sensed discouragement in my soul. I felt as if I had let my family down. I had a responsibility to take care of my people and provide a safe (and dry) place for them to live. I was failing. I had no courage. I had dis-courage.

> I was failing. I had no courage. I had dis-courage.

If you have ever been discouraged, you know the feeling. A state of discouragement is no place to live. It can paralyze us. In order to break free from discouragement, we have to dig deep.

IDENTIFY THE STRONGHOLD

Life requires courage. In order to gain

courage, we identify the stronghold by asking the "Why?" questions. For this example, let's say we are discouraged because we have a large, unexpected repair bill (like a car repair bill, a medical bill, or a bill for a new roof).

Question: **Why** are you discouraged?
Answer: Because I have a debt that I owe and I'm not sure I can pay it.

Question: **Why** does that bother you?
Answer: I feel irresponsible.

Question: **Why** do you feel irresponsible?
Answer: Because I don't have the money to pay for this.

Question: **Why** does that bother you?
Answer: Because it makes me feel like I am a bad person.

As we continue, we are getting closer to the stronghold. In this case, the stronghold would likely be something like, "Because I don't have the money to pay this bill, I am a bad person."

TRUTH THE STRONGHOLD

Once we find the stronghold, we apply the truth of scripture to it. In this case, we are looking for what the Bible says about us as a person. Again, a great way to search for verses of encouragement is to use Google or a Bible app.

CAPTURE THOUGHTS

Once we apply truth to the discouragement stronghold, we expect the enemy to bring other thoughts to our minds.

- "You will never have enough money to meet all your needs."
- "You are irresponsible."
- "You are an embarrassment to God."

We capture those thoughts by thinking about what we are thinking about. We grab them and hold on to them.

HAND IT TO JESUS

With our captured thought in hand, we give them to Jesus. This may be as simple as a prayer or as aggressive as writing our angry thoughts and putting them in the God box (see chapter 1).

FROM DISCOURAGEMENT TO
COURAGE TO FREEDOM

They both sat in my office. Husband and wife. Their words were calculated. There was no laughter. Small talk was not needed. A day earlier she was caught having an affair. He was devastated. She was ashamed. Discouragement was thick. There was one primary question which had to be answered: "Do you have the courage to put this marriage back together?"

> "Do you have the courage to put this marriage back together?"

After one of our worship services, a young man approached me. He was sick of his pornography addiction. As he talked, he expressed his discouragement. He had been trying to tame the cravings but had failed again and again. In order to win this battle, he would need courage.

They had dated since high school. Their relationship had started out well. Over time, he slowly turned abusive. At first the abuse was verbal; he was both controlling and condemning.

Occasionally, the abuse would turn physical. She was discouraged and in danger. Would she have the courage to end the relationship?

We all deal with discouragement. Maybe you have a situation right now which is leaving you full of discouragement. In order to dismantle the discouragement, we run it through the DITCH system. However, we don't simply want to get rid of discouragement; we want to replace it with courage. If we do, the next time the situation comes around (and it probably will) we can face it with courage.

"Discourage" literally means "no courage." In order for discouragement to turn to courage, we are going to need to take some action. The Bible gives us some instructions on how we can turn discourage into courage, and ultimately to freedom. It might not be easy, but it is possible.

Let's spend some time exploring Judges 4 in the Old Testament. I suggest you read the chapter on your own, but for now, allow me to summarize the happenings. The people of Israel had again disobeyed God. As a punishment, God allowed them to be captured by a guy named Jabin. Jabin appointed a man named Sisera as a leader of his army. Under the leadership of Sisera, the people of Israel were treated with cruelty for two decades.

Israel, in a twenty-year run of discouragement, cried out to God. God sent them a leader named Deborah. She made a plan to break Israel free from the discouragement. Deborah called for an Israelite named Barak and instructed him to rally some Israelite fighters and make an attack. Barak is full of more discouragement than courage. As a response, he stated that he would go but only if Deborah came with him. Deborah agreed, and they both made an attack. When they did, Sisera went on the run. During his escape, Sisera came to a tent and met a woman named Jael. He didn't realize that Jael was an Israelite (and thus his enemy). Sisera entered the tent and exhausted from the fight, fell asleep. Jael was a woman tired of the discouragement. In a dramatic move (insert climatic movie score here), she carefully walked up to Sisera and . . . well, I'm getting ahead of myself. We will come back around to her dramatic actions at the end of the chapter.

I'll sum up Judges 4 like this: In order for Israel to be free, God had to move the Israelites from discouragement to courage. The same is true with you and me. In order to be free, we are going to have to take the path to courage. Let's dive deeper in the story. As we do, we will uncover five steps which will take us from discouragement to courage to freedom.

Step #1: Listen

"Now Deborah, a *prophet*, the wife of Lappidoth, was leading Israel at that time. She held court under the Palm of Deborah between Ramah and Bethel in the hill country of Ephraim, and the Israelites went up to her to have their disputes decided. She sent for Barak son of Abinoam from Kedesh in Naphtali and said to him, "*The Lord, the God of Israel, commands you:* 'Go, take with you ten thousand men of Naphtali and Zebulun and lead them up to Mount Tabor" (Judges 4:4-6; emphasis mine).

When the Bible uses the term "prophet," it is describing someone whose primary job is to listen to what the Lord says. Before a prophet speaks to the people and says, "Thus sayeth the Lord . . ." He needs to know what the Lord sayeth. The only way he knows what the Lord is saying is by listening to Him.

As we step toward courage, it is important to listen to the Lord. He will tell us which battle to fight. When we become discouraged, we either have no idea what we are supposed to fight, or we have so many battles that we don't know where to start. By praying, God will help us choose which battles we need to fight.

Sitting in the back of a plane, I found myself discouraged. I was flying home after a week of work at a partner church in Haiti. I was saddened by the poverty and injustice that I saw in Haiti. On top of that, I was discouraged by the oppression in Africa. In addition, I was frustrated because I wanted to try to fix everything, but I didn't have the ability. I felt like if I said "yes" to Haiti, I would be saying "no" to Africa. If I said "yes" to Africa, I would be saying "no" to Haiti. Praying through my discouragement, I fell silent. That's when I felt the Lord give me direction. "You invest in Haiti.

I will call others to invest in Africa." The clear call of God moved me from discouragement to courage.

One of the most overlooked ways that we hear from God is through prayer. Most of the time we make quick prayers on the run.

- "God, help them."
- "Jesus, heal them."
- "God, help me in the interview."
- "Jesus, I need to get a good grade on this test."
- "God, I could use some favor here."

We close with an, "Amen," and move on. But an often-overlooked element is listening. Prayer is a two-way conversation. When is the last time that you prayed by listening? For the past year I have been ending my prayer times with listening. "Lord, thanks for listening to me. Now I want to pause and listen to You." I stop. And listen. Sometimes the Lord brings a situation or a person to mind. Sometimes He imprints even more deeply the scripture I just read (my prayer times are typically

> Prayer is a two-way conversation.

after I have spent time in the Bible). Sometimes I don't hear much. After a few minutes, I end my prayer time, but I do not end my listening. When I am at my best (which is not always), I am constantly listening during the day. Just yesterday, I heard a friend mention something that caught my attention. I believe that the Lord used the words of my friend to speak to me. If I had not been constantly listening, I would have missed the Lord's voice.

If you are new to listening to the voice of God, don't be frustrated. The more you chase Him, the more you will hear from Him. Like any discipline, it will take some time to develop. The best place to start hearing from Him is through the Bible. The Holy Spirit penned the words of Scripture and the same Holy Spirit that lives in you wants to bring those verses alive so that you can hear from God. In my previous book, *Soul Coma*, I write about a simple system (Life Journaling) which has helped thousands of people hear from God through Scripture.

When He was on this earth, Jesus spent considerable time listening to the Father. As a matter of fact, He would not make a move unless

He heard instructions from God. He would not speak unless He first heard. Here is how Jesus described His listening:

> So Jesus said, "When you have lifted up the Son of Man, then you will know that I am he and that I do nothing on my own but speak just what the Father has taught me" (John 8:28).

If you are ready to replace discouragement with courage, before you start making some rash actions, stop. Seek the Lord. Listen for His voice. Wait for His instructions. He will give you the direction you need.

Once we have listened and heard some clear direction from the Lord, we move into the next step. This is where the rubber meets the road. Up until now, our movement towards courage has been about listening. It is now time to take a deep breath and move into action.

> Seek the Lord. Listen for His voice. Wait for His instructions. He will give you the direction you need.

Step #2: Lead out

In your journey to freedom, you are going to have to lead out. Because this is your fight, others cannot fight it for you. In our story of the courage of Israel, our friend Barak desires freedom, but he does not want to lead out. Listen to how Scripture recorded the story.

> "She [Deborah] sent for Barak son of Abinoam from Kedesh in Naphtaliand said to him, 'The Lord, the God of Israel, commands you: 'Go, take with you ten thousand men of Naphtali and Zebulun and lead them up to Mount Tabor. I will lead Sisera, the commander of Jabin's army, with his chariots and his troops to the Kishon River and give him into your hands.''Barak said to her, 'If you go with me, I will go; but if you don't go with me, I won't go'" (Judges 4:6-8).

Are you kidding me? Here is the leader of Israel asking Barak to change the course of history and break a 20-year journey of discouragement. She asks him to lead out. Instead of taking a deep breath and mustering the courage, he says (in my paraphrase) "Well, I guess I will go, but only if you hold my hand."

Come on, Barak. Step up. Grow a spine. Get some men. Go and mow down your oppressors. Win the day. Okay, easy for me to say, but the point is this: God calls Barak to lead out. He had a battle to fight, and God was asking him to engage. He could recruit people to fight with him, but he was called to lead in the fight.

God is calling you to lead your fight to freedom. The people around you can fight with you, but they can't fight for you. It's your fight. They can't give you their courage. You are going to have to step up and lead the fight. But, have no fear. If God is calling you to the battle, He will lead you through the fight. Let that soak in. If God calls you to

> If God calls you to it, He will lead you through it.

it, He will lead you through it. Stop doubting His call. Stop second-guessing His instructions. You know what He has called you to do. Take a leap of faith. Grab some Holy-Spirit-induced courage and get the job done. What's the worst that could happen? Of course, the addiction looks big. Sure, the fight looks impossible. It's true that you failed at your last three attempts. Lead out anyway. Do you really think that God would call you to lead only to watch you suffer?

After we listen to the Lord and lead out, the journey is far from over. Because the Lord is with us in the journey to freedom, He will offer us some reminders along the way.

Step #3: Look

I love this part of the journey. As we step out in courageous faith, we are going to doubt. Because our courage is at risk of turning back to discouragement, we have to keep our eyes open for what the Lord is doing. Deborah had great courage in the middle of the journey because she looked for God.

> "Then Deborah said to Barak, 'Go! This is the day the Lord has given Sisera into your hands. *Has not the Lord gone ahead of you?*' So Barak went down Mount Tabor, with ten thousand men following him" (Judges 4:14; emphasis mine).

As we lead out, we need to look around. When we do, we often see that the Lord has already gone ahead of us. We see His fingerprints. That is, He has already been working in people and in circumstances. By looking and seeing His actions, it gives us even more courage.

Last week, I talked to my friend Pastor Ray Jones. Ray recounted to me a situation in his life where he *listened*, *led out*, and had to *look for God*. As he told the story, my jaw was on the floor.

Through a series of unfortunate circum-stances, Ray found himself a single dad of two teenaged boys. As if working a full-time job and raising boys alone weren't enough, Ray was deeply lonely. Prayer was a constant part of his life, and many times he asked the Lord for a woman with which he could share his life. Ray made it a point of continually asking God for what he desired. Most of the time the Lord fell silent, except on one particularly discouraging evening.

As Ray tells the story, he put his boys to bed and, as was routine, spoke to the Lord. (Ray actually says that he was "complaining to the Lord.") Despite his discouragement, he again asked for a companion that he could share his life with. Ray sensed the Lord say, "Ray, I'm pleased with you." This was a bit of a shock to Ray. He (like most of us) always felt like he had to win God's approval. That statement, however, was not the most interesting thing Ray would hear that night. The Lord continued, "The greatest days for you are ahead, and I am going to send you a lady named Andrea to walk with you."

Over the next few days, Ray kept this to himself. He did know a woman named Andrea. They had met a few months earlier when she was on a mission trip that Ray was leading. Like you and me, Ray was probably wondering, *Did I hear correctly? Am I crazy? Did the Lord really speak, or was that my imagination?*

Ray was now at a point where he needed to look for the movement of the Lord. If Ray *heard* God right, then he should be able to *see* God moving. (God's moving should match His speaking.) Within the next eight days, Ray had seven different people say they felt like the name "Andrea" had come to mind when they thought of Ray. (Remember, Ray had not shared with anyone what he heard in his prayer time.) It appeared that God was up to something. Ray looked and saw the hand of the Lord moving.

After those eight days, God spoke to Ray again. You would think at this point God would tell Ray to speak with Andrea, ask her out on a date, and get this party rolling. But God clearly told Ray something different. "I want you to call Andrea and tell her you should be married." Ray was stunned. He took time and prayed about what he heard. And then he prayed again. And some more. A few evenings later, Ray picked up the phone and made the call.

Pause here. You have to know that my friend Ray is not some off-the-wall guy. He is someone just like you and me: a normal person trying to figure out what God is doing and looking hard for His movement. Now, back to our story.

Andrea picked up the phone, and she and Ray began a conversation. After three hours, Ray finally got to the point. His words were clear. "Listen, this is going to sound strange to you, but God has put a love in my heart for you, and He has spoken to me, and I believe we should be married . . . and maybe we could, like, have a date sometime."

> After three hours, Ray finally got to the point.

Woah! Wait! Hang on, Ray. Did you just pick up the phone and ask a girl you have barely met to marry you? Indeed, he did.

As Ray reports, he hung up the phone, and for the next several hours he paced back and forth in his room. His mind was spinning as he thought of how he had made perhaps the dumbest move of his life and how Andrea would likely never speak to him again.

Nearly two weeks went by. No word from Andrea. One evening Ray was at church getting ready for a live worship recording that he was producing. Pretty close to start time, people were crowding in the church, and Ray was deep in a thousand details. Ray's son came and found him backstage. His son held out a note. "Dad, this is for you." Ray informed his son that he was in the middle of a huge production and that it would have to wait. "Dad, this is from Andrea." Ray stopped in his tracks. He opened the note.

> I'm here tonight. The Lord had
> already told me that you were going
> to ask me. The answer is "yes."
> - Andrea

Three decades later, Ray and Andrea are still together, with a story that never gets old. Looking back, Ray would tell you that he was discouraged. But he used that discouragement to listen to the Lord to lead out, and to look for His hand along the way. At each step, Ray was filled with a little more courage. I have a feeling that when Ray started to doubt, God would send him another sign, another glimpse that He was at work. As a result, Ray would have a little more courage.

I believe one of the reasons God allows us to see His work is so that we can stay full of courage. Courage leaks, and once we are on the journey, we may start to doubt. Don't let your courage turn to discouragement. Listen to these words from Deuteronomy:

"Be strong and courageous. Do not be afraid or terrified because of them, for the Lord your God goes with you; he will never leave you nor forsake you" (Deuteronomy 31:6).

God is with you. You will see His work. Oh, and don't think that He will leave you. That's not His nature. As a matter of fact, in His last audible words, Jesus reminds us of His presence with us.

"... And surely I am with you always, to the very end of the age" (Matthew 28:20).

Friend, if you listen to Him and lead out, make sure you look around. If you see Him at work, you know you are on the right track. When you see His fingerprints, allow yourself to be filled with even more courage. You are well on the way to freedom. Keep going. As you do, make sure you take this next crucial step of freedom.

Step #4: Lock arms with others

When Deborah instructed Barak to lead, she didn't expect him to go solo. She expected that he would recruit some men to fight alongside him.

"She sent for Barak son of Abinoam from Kedesh in Naphtali and said to him, 'The Lord, the God of Israel, commands you: 'Go, *take with you ten thousand men* of Naphtali and Zebulun *and lead them* up to Mount Tabor"
(Judges 4:6; emphasis mine).

If you are like me, you are terrible at asking for help. Maybe it's pride, or maybe it's that we don't want to bother people, but, for whatever reason, we would rather go it alone than reach out. The problem with that approach is that it makes freedom even more elusive. We were made to live in community. We were

> **We were made to live in community.**

made to celebrate joys and hardships with each other. When called on for a great task, we are expected to enlist the help of those around us. I am slowly learning this.

I'll spare you the details, but several years ago I experienced the greatest crisis of my life. As a family we were realizing significant health issues which touched every area of life (financial, relational, spiritual). During that time, I led a small group of men through a study of how to be better followers of Christ. Every Thursday at 6:00 a.m. we met, studied, and shared our battles. In truth, they shared their battles. I was their leader. As such, I believed that I was supposed to model unquestionable courage. Looking back, I realize how ridiculous that was. During one early morning session, I cracked the door to my life just a bit. I let them in on some of the struggles. They must have sensed that I was in the fight alone. Later that week I got a text from one of the men.

"Scot, this is Michael. What can the men and I do for you?"

"Hey, Michael, thanks for reaching out. I appreciate you thinking of me, but I'm good."

"Yea, so, the guys and I were were talking. What can we do? What do you need done?"

"Man, you are so generous, but I'm not really sure. We are good. Really."

"Yea, well how about some stuff around the house. What have you been wanting to do that you can't get done because your life is crazy right now?"

"Aw, you know, there is always stuff that needs done, but it's nothing that I can't handle."

"Make a list. The group and I will be at your house next Saturday at 10:00am. We will knock out everything on the list. See you then."

I started getting tears in my eyes. I *did* need the help. I was exhausted by trying to go it alone.

I wanted help, but I hated to ask. That following Saturday the crew showed up. In two hours, they knocked out projects that would have taken me months.

Beyond the physical work that they got done, they did a spiritual work in me. I didn't feel like I was alone in the fight. They reminded me that part of the call to freedom is to lock arms with those around us. We are called to lead our own battles, but we are not called to fight them alone. In your fight, enlist some friends. Take the hill together. They care for you more than you can imagine.

> We are called to lead our own battles, but we are not called to fight them alone.

Let's review. On our journey from discouragement to courage to freedom, we take the following steps:

- Listen

- Lead

- Look

- Lock arms

We have one final step. This final step is the most exciting step: we must liquidate. (Have you noticed that each of these steps start with the letter "L?")

Step #5: Liquidate

When I speak of liquidating, I'm not talking about a store having a liquidation sale. I'm talking about something more violent. According to old man Webster, liquidate is defined as "to do away with especially by killing."[13]

God did not ask Deborah and Barak to negotiate with the opponent. He did not instruct them to send a strongly worded letter. He didn't call them to offer a warning. God wanted the enemy liquidated. He wanted them dead.

Like many other stories in the Bible, this reads like the score of a great movie. Let me catch you up. Barak and his boys attacked Sisera. As a result, Sisera's men were on the run. Worn out and delirious from battle, Sisera saw a tent belonging to a woman named Jael. What he didn't know was that Jael was an Israelite. Cue the sweeping movie score; this is the scene we have been waiting for.

DISCOURAGEMENT: From Discouragement to Courage to Freedom

"Jael went out to meet Sisera and said to him, 'Come, my lord, come right in. Don't be afraid.' So he entered her tent, and she covered him with a blanket.

'I'm thirsty,' he said. 'Please give me some water.' She opened a skin of milk, gave him a drink, and covered him up.

'Stand in the doorway of the tent,' he told her. 'If someone comes by and asks you, 'Is anyone in there?' say 'No.''

But Jael, Heber's wife, picked up a tent peg and a hammer   and went quietly to him while he lay fast asleep, exhausted. She drove the peg through his temple into the ground, and he died" (Judges 4:18-21).

Whew! Don't pick a fight with Jael. She caught the vision. In one tremendous act, she moved from discouraged to courage to freedom. The oppressor was dead. Defunct. Expired. Liquidated.

Lest you think this is gruesome and a little over the top, be reminded that there are some things in this life that have to die. I am not suggesting we put the hit out on a person. I am saying there may be some thoughts, activities, actions, or even relationships that you must kill. The only way to walk in complete freedom is to kill what is trying to kill you.

I have a friend who became so discouraged with his pornography addiction that he decided to kill it. He confessed to his wife. He confessed to his small group. He put ridiculous restrictions on his computer. (The man cannot even google the word "pants" without his wife getting an email alert.) He is now living in freedom. To get there, he had to gather his courage and make the kill.

Over the years, several discouraged people have come into my office with problems. They are seeking freedom. It might be a relationship strain, an addiction, a bad habit, or thousands of other hang-ups. Like I stated at the beginning of the chapter, I want to know if they have courage. But I need to know something else. The answer to this question will determine if they will walk into freedom. "Do you have enough courage to kill what is trying to kill you?"

What about you? Do you have the courage to kill? Are you willing to kill what is trying to take you down? If so, do not back down. Do not go easy. Get aggressive. Go on a mission to destroy. In doing so, you will be on the same mission that Jesus was on. He clearly stated His mission when He said "... The reason the Son of God appeared was to destroy the devil's work" (1 John 3:8).

If you find yourself in a place of discouragement, it may be that the Lord wants to use that feeling in order to take you to courage and ultimately to freedom. For many of us, this is a daily battle. While the battle may be constant, the presence of Jesus is constant as well. He will help us listen, lead out, look, lock arms with others, and liquidate. Imagine what it will be like when you look back and see from where you have come. Imagine remembering your discouragement and how it launched you into a life of freedom!

Don't stay in discouragement. *DITCH* it. Let the Lord use it as you find your way out. Every journey begins with one small step. Take it. And as you do, know that you are not alone on your journey to freedom.

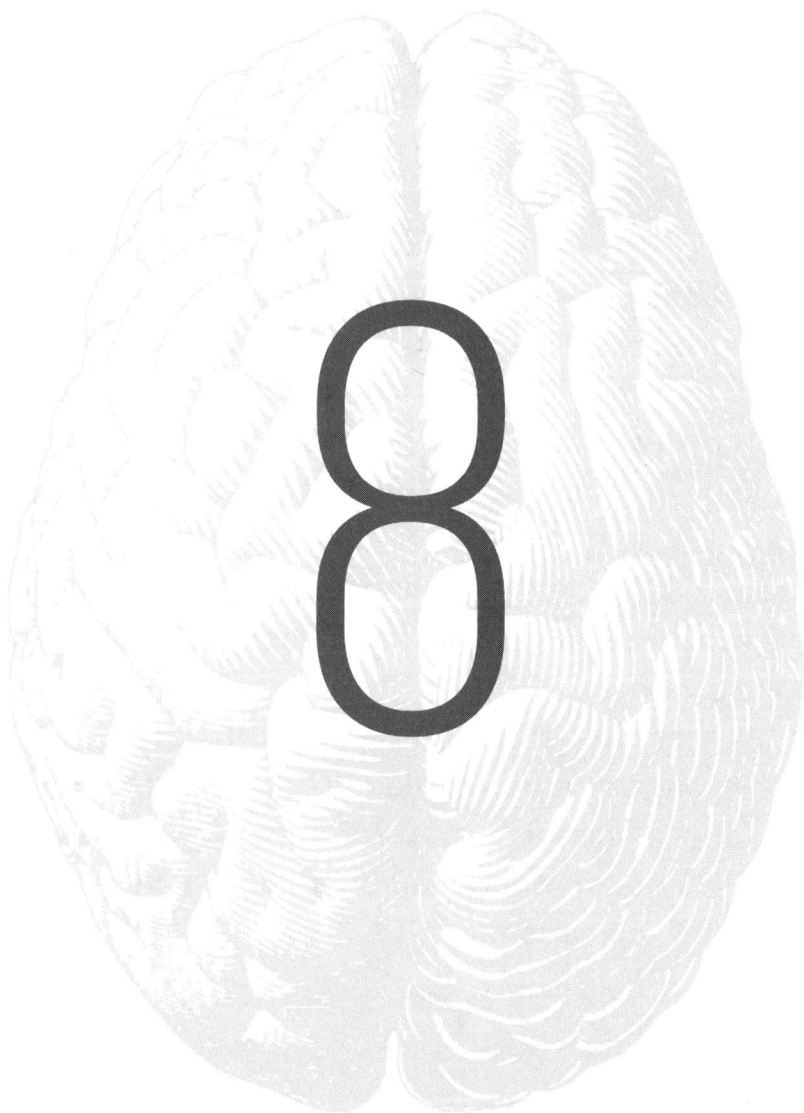

8

DITCH the Apathy

DETERMINE THE EMOTION

It was probably the closest thing to road rage I had ever experienced. One cloudy afternoon in a Wal-Mart parking lot, I found myself face-to-face with a man who was fuming over what he thought was my lack of driving skills. Moments earlier I had inadvertently failed to stop at a stop sign. To be fair, it was a weird intersection and I assumed it was a four-way stop. It was not. When an oncoming driver saw me in the intersection, he had to slow down. Since he was far away, there was little danger. The chance of an accident was slim to none. Granted, I was in the wrong, but I figured no harm, no foul. The other driver did not share my same perspective.

The offended driver sped up and chased me through the lot. Once close, he pulled in front of my truck, forcing me to stop. Throwing his car in park, he walked straight to my door. I rolled down the window. He unloaded in a verbal barrage. Clearly, he needed to inform me of my mistake as well as his expertise. He was rude, belligerent, arrogant, and disrespectful. Me? I didn't care. I don't mean that I didn't listen to what he said, and I worked hard to not let it affect me, I mean I didn't care a shred. I could not have cared less about the situation, the man, the intersection, his anger, or my mistake. There was a simple reason that I was not bothered: I was numb.

Our family had been walking through a dark time. So dark that I will not relive it here. Trust me when I say that the struggle was all-encompassing, much bigger than rolling through a stop sign. In the middle of that struggle, I simply did not care about much of anything. I was void of motivation and full of apathy.

Apathy literally means "without feeling." It's the feeling when you know that you should get out of bed, but you don't want to. When you should study for the test, but you are unmotivated. When you know you should try, but it seems so hard to move. Apathy can leave us stuck in a rut. Stay in the apathy rut long enough, and it can be paralyzing. The comfort of doing nothing seems like a better option than risking and failing.

Psychology Today reports that apathy is an attitude of, ". . . indifference . . . unconcern . . . unresponsiveness . . . detachment . . . and dispassion. Such an attitude saps you of so much energy that you feel lethargic, listless, and enervated—almost too "paralyzed" to act—and certainly without the will to do so."[14]

Apathy is real. When apathy hits, we need to deconstruct the feeling and run it through the DITCH method in order to see if we can wrestle it down.

IDENTIFY THE STRONGHOLD

Identifying the apathetic stronghold is harder than most emotions simply because of the energy required. DITCHing our emotions requires intensity, and apathy steals our energy. Take a deep breath. Harness some extra motivation and start asking the "Why?" questions. For this example, let's say we are apathetic toward a school or work project. We just can't seem to find the motivation to do the work.

Question: *Why* are you apathetic?
Answer: I don't know, I just am.

Question: That's an apathetic answer, so I'll ask it again, "**Why** are you apathetic?"

Answer: I'm just not motivated to do the project.

Question: **Why** are you not motivated?

Answer: Because it's a ton of work.

Question: **Why** does that bother you?

Answer: Because I could do all this work and the project could still be bad.

Question: **Why** does that matter?

Answer: Because if the project is bad I will have wasted my time and will have failed.

Question: Which is worse, wasting your time or failing?

Answer: Failing. I don't want to be a failure.

Question: So, if you fail at this project you would consider yourself a failure?

Answer: Yes.

Boom! The stronghold is clear: If we attempt the project and fail, we are a failure. Our minds are using apathy (and fear) to lie and keep us trapped.

TRUTH THE STRONGHOLD

Once we find the stronghold, we apply the truth of scripture to it. In this case, we are looking for what the Bible says about us as a person. Again, a great way to search for verses of encouragement is to use Google or any number of Bible software programs, a Bible concordance, or the Bible itself.

CAPTURE THOUGHTS

Once we put the smack down on the lies that trigger anger, we expect the enemy to bring other thoughts back at us:

- "What makes you think you can accomplish this? You are not smart enough."
- "You will be made fun of."
- "You are in way over your head."
- "You failed last time. What makes you think this time will be any different?"

We capture those thoughts by thinking about what we are thinking about. We grab them and hold on to them.

HAND IT TO JESUS

With our captured thoughts in hand, we give them to Jesus. This may be as simple as a prayer or as aggressive as writing our angry thoughts and putting them in the God box (see chapter 1).

FROM APATHY TO IDENTITY

I am convinced that we are the most apathetic when we forget who we are. Said another way, we are most apathetic when we forget our identity. Let me illustrate with a story.

Sixth grade, 1981. Not exactly the pinnacle of my success. I had a few friends but was mostly on the outside of the cool circle. I'm not sure if it was my off-brand tennis shoes, bright red hair, freckles, pudgy build, acne, lack of smarts, or a combination of them all, but let's just say I was not the most popular with anyone, especially the ladies. As if sixth grade doesn't have enough struggles, I was also trying to find out who I was. My identity became clear one fateful day in early spring.

For some unknown reason, I had collected enough courage to pass "Emily" a note. (I have changed the name in order to protect the innocent from embarrassment.) I had written a carefully constructed letter and passed it to a friend who passed it to a friend who passed it to Emily. The note was simple and to the point.

> I like you. Do you like me?
> Yes
> No (Please circle one)
> Maybe
>   Scot

I waited for the return of said letter. I knew the risk was high. I was fairly certain of the outcome. The letter would likely be returned with a circle around the "no." I was used to the rejection (it came with the freckles and ridiculous feathering in my thick red hair). I waited.

Sometime later that morning, the note made its way back into my hand. I could not believe my eyes. A circle around "yes." What? Was this some kind of mistake? Was this a cruel joke? Could this actually be true? I had my friends run a quick confirmation. According to Emily and her group of friends, it was true. Emily liked me. She liked *me*.

Later that afternoon, I was in a vehicle with our teacher and four other students (we had won some sort of prize, and our teacher was taking us to lunch). On the car ride, my mind started slipping to its usual rut of apathy. *Nobody likes me. I will never be enough. School is hard. I'm a nobody.* Then I remembered the note from earlier. Emily liked me. I was not a nobody; I was a somebody. I had a new identity: I was someone who Emily liked.

Friend, that situation took place almost 40 years ago, and I can still tell you where I was sitting in the car when I became fully aware that Emily liked me. I can take you to the exact place on the road where we were driving when the realization hit me. My identity changed in that one moment. I thought differently. I talked differently. I walked differently. My apathy was in the rearview. I was motivated and energized, all because I knew who I was. I was someone that Emily liked.

Our apathy is tied to our identity. When we realize that we are liked (and loved), apathy is diffused, and motivation is ignited. The single greatest truth to lead us out of apathy is this: We are loved and liked by God.

Read that again. Don't let that pass you by. You are loved. You are liked. You may not believe it. You may think you don't deserve it (none of us does). You may think you have not earned it (none of us has), but do not flush the truth; you are loved and liked by God.

Somewhere along the way, we have forgotten who we are. Our identity has eroded. As a result, we slip into apathy. In order to ditch the apathy, allow me to remind us of who we are.

If you are a follower of Jesus, here is your identity:

1. You are constantly wanted

As I write this, Stephanie and I have been married for more than 30 years. Much of our schedule is filled with travel. Over the course of three decades we have come up with what we call the "two-week rule." As a general practice, we will not be away from each other for more than two weeks. We find that anything beyond 14 days creates a strain on our relationship and does not keep us emotionally healthy. Truth is, even after 30 years, we still like hanging around each other. We *want* to be with each other.

Imagine I am on a trip, and after 10 days, I call Steph. "Hey, I really miss your cooking. I also miss you doing my laundry; I have a bunch of dirty clothes. Oh, and I miss you keeping my calendar straight." I'm pretty sure when I returned home, I would be sleeping on the couch. Why? Because I told Steph that I wanted her because of what she could do for me. Not because I loved her just for just being herself.

Do not ever think that the Lord wants you because of what you can do *for* Him. Honestly, what could you ever do for God that He could not do for Himself? He wants you - constantly - because He loves you. You are His. The Psalmist reminds us of this when he writes,

> "Know that the Lord is God. It is he who made us, and *we are his*; we are his people, the sheep of his pasture" (Psalm 100:3; emphasis mine).

The Apostle Paul tells us the same thing when he says,

> "If we live, we live for the Lord; and if we die, we die for the Lord. So, whether we live or die, *we belong to the Lord*" (Romans 14:8; emphasis mine).

You are His child. God wants His kids, just like I want my kids. Speaking of which, Steph and I have two amazing daughters. Over

> ## You are His child.

the course of the years, we have instituted one of my favorite activities: "snuggle time." Snuggle time is simple. Grab a blanket, hit the couch, flip on a movie, and snuggle. As my kids have gotten older, snuggle time is less frequent. But I hope they remember what I have told them on occasion. "When you get older, you won't want to snuggle with old dad so much, but that's alright. Just know that you always have a place right here, next to me." I wanted my girls to know one thing: They are constantly wanted by their daddy. My daughters should never wonder if their father wants them. And neither should you.

Your Heavenly Father lives in a constant state of wanting you. The story of the cross is the story of His great desire for you. He desired you with such fervency that He made the unthinkable sacrifice for you. You, friend, are a child of the King. And our Father wants His kids, constantly.

2. You are not alone

"Where can I go from your Spirit? Where can I flee from your presence? If I go up to the heavens, you are there; if I make my bed in the depths, you are there.

If I rise on the wings of the dawn if I settle on the far side of the sea, even there your hand will guide me, your right hand will hold me fast" (Psalm 139:7-10).

I was lost. Physically lost. And alone. And a bit scared.

I had taken a day away at a secluded prayer center. I settled into one of the cabins and used the day to read, pray, and seek the Lord. After a few hours, I decided a walk in the woods was in order. It was mid-afternoon as I set out to get some fresh air. On my way into the woods, I was met by two dogs who lived at the prayer center.

Large, mangy mutts, one named Goodness, the other Mercy. (Seriously, I'm not making this up.) Goodness, Mercy, and I set out on a trek through the woods. I'm not the best with directions, but how hard could it be to keep your way in the woods? Evidently harder than I thought.

After a couple hours of walking and praying through the forest, I decided it was time to make my way back to the cabin, get packed up, and head home. I looked up from the path. "Um . . . which way is the cabin? Do I head back where I came? Do I keep going straight ahead? Am I even headed in the right direction?" I asked Goodness and Mercy for directions. They just gave me the confused dog look (you know, they turn their head and look at you like "whaaaaat?"). I spent the next hour focused on getting back to the cabin. At one point, I was pretty sure I was going in circles. "Did I pass that same stump earlier?" I was lost.

Making a plan for escape, I decided to walk out of the woods toward what I hoped was a paved road. I figured that once I found a road, I could make my way back to the prayer center. After much effort, I exited the woods and discovered a road. I looked around. Nothing was familiar. Zero.

I could not tell north from south. I recognized no landmarks. I needed help. This was in the time before cell phones, so I was totally on my own. Well, not totally alone. I turned toward my four-legged companions. They took a final look at me, turned around, and ran off. Evidently, Goodness and Mercy would not follow me all the days of my life.

In the distance, I saw a house. I made my way there. Near the house was an older gentleman. When I asked how to get back to the prayer center, he cocked his head and gave me the same look that I had seen from the dogs earlier. Perfect. This guy had no idea. It was at that moment I realized I was not only lost, I was alone.

Have you ever felt alone? Of course, we all have. But the crazy fact is that we are never solo. Even if we feel like we are isolated, we are not. In Mathew 28 Jesus says ". . . And surely I am with you always, to the very end of the age" (Matthew 28:19). From His lips comes this promise: You are not alone.

As a matter of fact, for Jesus to leave you alone, He would have to violate who He is. One of the names for Jesus is "Immanuel," which literally means "God with us" (Matthew 1:23). His very nature is that He is an ever-present God. We may feel alone. We may be physically alone, but we are never really alone.

Part of our identity is that we are constantly in the presence of Jesus. We are not alone. We never will be. Let that fact shake us out of our apathy. We are in the constant presence of the Father, Son, and Holy Spirit.

3. You are fearless

"I know what it is to be in need, and I know what it is to have plenty. I have learned the secret of being content in any and every situation, whether well fed or hungry, whether living in plenty or in want. *I can do all this through him* who gives me strength" (Philippians 4:12-13; emphasis mine).

Memphis, 1978. I was with my dad in a place where we should not have been. My dad owned his own trucking business and, as such, would often deliver freight across the US. On occasion, he would let one of the kids go with him. On this particular trip, we found ourselves broken down in Memphis, Tennessee. Through the recommendation of a friend, we had taken my dad's semi to a tire shop in the inner city. As they were working on the truck, Dad and I decided to walk a few blocks away and grab a sandwich. Mistake.

As we made our way toward lunch, a man approached us. In his hand was a knife. Moving the knife toward us he said, "Hey! Hey!" After a few moments, we realized that he was not trying to rob us, he was inebriated and wanted us to buy his knife. Dad declined the transaction, and we headed toward lunch.

Back at the shop, my dad talked to one of the employees. "We were headed to get a sandwich and a guy pulled a knife on us. The whole thing kind of rattled my son." My dad was only half right. Someone pulled a knife on us, but I was not rattled. As a matter of fact, I don't remember being afraid at all. Maybe I should have been. After all, I was a nine-year-old kid in a neighborhood where I should not have been. I had been approached by a guy with a knife. He was drunk. He could have stabbed me. He could have robbed me. He could have kidnapped me.

But I was not afraid. I was genuinely without fear at that moment. That's right, my nine-year-old self was fearless when approached by a knife-wielding drunk man in Memphis. How could I be fearless? Simple - Dad was there. The presence of my father caused me to be fearless.

Our Heavenly Father is always present. Because He is always present, we are fearless. It's not that we are to "act" fearless or "pretend" to be fearless. Fearless is who we are — it is our identity. And it is our identity because of Jesus.

> You are fearless.

Look at what Paul said: "I can do all this through him who gives me strength" (Philippians 4:13). Paul is fearless because of the presence of Christ. Do you have Christ? If so, "fearless" is part of your identity. It is who you are. After a while, you realize that what is coming against you is smaller than the One who is in you. Step up. You have nothing to fear. You are fearless.

The fact that we are fearless is tied to another reminder of our identity. Don't push back on this next one. Lean into it. Let it erode apathy and bring you to identity. Here is our next reminder:

4. You are a carrier of greatness

"You, dear children, are from God and
have overcome them, because *the
one who is in you is greater* than
the one who is in the world"
(1 John 4:4; emphasis mine).

My friend Jim loves Jesus. He also likes an occasional round of trash talking. Even though he is older, Jim still loves to play basketball with a group of young guys. When he does, the mocking starts. After a successful layup in the face of an opponent, Jim is known to literally take out his AARP card and say, "Son, do you realize a senior citizen just schooled you?" I love this guy.

One day, Jim found himself in a potentially violent situation. In the middle of a basketball game, two teenage young men started to fight. Jim, frustrated at their stupidity (and the interruption of his weekly exercise), did the unthinkable. He stepped between the two men. As Jim tells the story, "That's when it got interesting." Evidently the young men offered to provide to Jim what they had intended for each other. The two enemies now united and started threatening Jim. It was apparent that a fight was about to break out. An AARP card wouldn't be much good this round.

One of the young men stepped to Jim's face. "What you got, old man?" Silence. Tension They asked again, "Hey! What you got, old man?"

Jim looked them in the eye. He paused. When he spoke, he was calm and clear.

"What do I have? What do I have? Well, what I have is a promise that says the One who is in me is greater than the one who is in you. And every now and then I like to put that promise to the test."

Mic. Drop. My man Jim just pulled off a Clint Eastwood moment. Somehow the situation diffused and there was no violence. The crazy thing? Jim actually believes what he said. He believes that he is a carrier of greatness. And so are you. The same Holy Spirit that raised Christ from the dead is in you (Romans 8:11). You carry greatness.

When the enemy comes against you and says, "Ha, what you got now?" You can reply "Well, I have a promise that says that the One inside of me is greater than you, and sometimes I like to put that promise to the test."

Can you feel the apathy draining as you realize who you are? Chin up. Shoulders back. Straighten the spine. You house greatness. And nothing can defeat you.

5. You are undefined by your past

"Therefore, if anyone is in Christ, *the new creation has come*: The old has gone, the new is here!" (1 Cor 5:17; emphasis mine)

I find that much of our apathy is tied to the defeat that we carry from the past. We remember our failings and our sins and think "I have a track record of defeat. Why even try again?" I'll tell you exactly why you should try again: You are not defined by your past; you are defined by your Christ.

> You are not defined by your past; you are defined by your Christ.

Sometimes a person will come to me and say, "Scot, I saw a guy at church on Sunday. I know some stuff about this guy. When I knew him years ago, he was an addict, and he wrecked his marriage." This same person will give me a list of failures of the other person and then he will typically end by saying, "I just can't believe he is at church." My response is always the same. "That's the old man. What you are seeing is the new man."

If you are a follower of Jesus, your past is in your past. Sure, you probably have some consequences which have made their way into your present, but if Christ has forgiven you, you are new. Maybe you were a cheater, but that's the old you. Maybe you were an addict, but that's the old you. Maybe you were a hater, a gossip, a liar, a . . . whatever. But no more. Your past is in your past.

> "as far as the east is from the west,
> so far has he removed our
> transgressions from
> us" (Psalm 103:12).

Let's pause for a moment here. The Psalmist tells us that if we have confessed our sins, that God takes them far from us. How far? As far as the east is from the west. That got me thinking. "How far is the east from the west?"

On earth, the distance between east and west is approximately 12,450 miles.[15] So the author could be saying, "God has taken your past sins 12,450 miles away." But what if the author is not talking about the east-west distance of the earth? What if he is talking about the east-west distance of all creation? In that case, the distance between east and west would be, well, we don't know. We have not fully discovered all the universe. It is just big. Really big. The point is this: God has put a great distance between our sin and us. Whether it is 12,450 miles or infinity, our past sins are too far away to go visit. Leave them where they are. Your past is in the past. Do not let it define you.

And while I am on this little "sin-in-the-past" rant, let me remind us of this fact: If you have confessed the sins of your past, God has forgotten them. It's not that we wish He would forget them. It's not that we hope He forgets them. If we confess them, they are out of His mind.

"For I will forgive their wickedness and
will remember their sins no more"
(Hebrews 8:12).

If you pray, "God, you know that sin last week? I mean, I know I asked for forgiveness, but that sin, you know the one I am talking about?"

God will reply, "Your sin in the past? Nope! I do not know what you are talking about." He has chosen to forget your sins. If He has chosen to forget, so should you. Your sins are gone, As far as the east is from the west – gone. Gone from the mind of the Father and gone from our lives. We are left undefined by our past and defined only by our Christ. Come on! That *has* to fire y ou up!

Apathy is caused by a lack of identity. Our enemy would love for us to forget who we are. If he can make us apathetic, he can disarm us from our mission. Oh, but we know who we are. We are constantly wanted. We are not alone. We are fearless. We are carriers of greatness. And we are undefined by our past. Shake off the cobwebs. Wipe the sleep from your eyes. Take a good look at the Savior. Ditch the apathy and find out who you really are.

"Yet to all who did receive him, to those who believed in his name, he gave the right to become children of God" (John 1:12).

9

DITCH the Disappointment

DETERMINE THE EMOTION

I'm not sure what possessed me to run for 10th grade class president. Was it my popularity? Nope. Dashing good looks? No. Dynamic athleticism? Nyet. Superior intelligence? Negatory. Maybe it was that a pretty girl said, "You should run for class president." Or maybe it was a desperate attempt to feel like people liked me. For whatever reason, I signed up, and my political career began.

My campaign strategy consisted of poster board, markers, and some lame lettering. The marketing plan was simple: persuade people to vote for a guy they had never heard of. I soon found out that posters were not the only type of marketing that the 10th grade political system utilized. There was also a dreaded candidate debate. During a student body gathering, each person would have five minutes to introduce himself and explain why he was the best person for the job.

For my campaign speech, I decided to use humor. After all, everyone would vote for a president that could bring the funny, right? I'll save you the details of the train wreck that was my speech. Let's just say that I bombed. I don't mean that I was "not funny." I mean that I was terrible. Like just short of getting booed off the stage, terrible. I even had props. "Surely props would get a laugh," I thought. Crickets. Not even a chuckle. I started my speech as a potential candidate for class president. At the end of the speech, I had given myself and everyone in the room a crystal-clear look into the future: I would *not* be the next class president.

That glorious event took place around 1985. To this day, I can remember walking down from the stage and feeling a myriad of emotions. Near the top was the emotion of disappointment. I was disappointed in my speech, disappointed in my poster, and disappointed because no one would vote for me. Most of all, I was disappointed in myself (an emotion I had become all too familiar with).

Disappointment is defined as a "sadness or displeasure caused by the nonfulfillment of one's hopes or expectations."[16] I bet you know the feeling of disappointment. Maybe you have been disappointed with yourself. Maybe you have failed to live up to your own expectations. You may have bombed the test, blown the interview, or opened your mouth when you should have kept it closed.

Maybe someone else has disappointed you. Perhaps you got passed over for the promotion, or you didn't get into the university. Maybe your friends have treated you poorly, or maybe your father has not been as present as you had hoped.

Disappointment is a part of life but hidden behind the pain is a sometimes deeper issue that needs to be uncovered and healed. For this example, let's say that you find yourself deeply disappointed because you have been passed over for a job promotion. You worked hard, went the extra mile, and were certain that your efforts would be rewarded. In your mind, you had more skill, knowledge, and time in the company than anyone else. You were a shoo-in for the promotion. But, when the announcement was made, you were passed over. The decision left you deeply disappointed. So, let's deconstruct the emotion of disappointment.

IDENTIFY THE STRONGHOLD

Because disappointment can sometimes deplete our energy, we may have to work extra hard at identifying the stronghold. If we are not careful, we can throw ourselves a pity party.

- "Nobody thinks I am any good at my job."
- "I will never get ahead in this company."
- "Someone will always get the promotion before I will."

Shake that thinking off. Take a deep breath and start asking the "Why?" questions.

Question: **Why** are you disappointed?

Answer: Because I was passed over for the promotion, again.

Question: **Why** does that bother you?

Answer: It makes me feel like I am not worth anything to the company.

Question: **Why** do you think you are not worth anything to the company?

Answer: If they thought I was worth something to them, they would reward me with a promotion. They don't believe I have value.

Question: **Why** is it important that they see your value?

Answer: Because I want them to recognize how hard I work, and that I am worth something.

Question: So, if you work hard, then you are worth something?

Answer: Uhhhh . . .

We have found the stronghold: My value is based on what others think of my job performance.

TRUTH THE STRONGHOLD

Once we find the stronghold, we apply the truth of scripture to it. In this case, we are looking for what the Bible says about our value. Again, a great way to search for verses of encouragement is to use Google, Bible software programs, or Bible study tools.

CAPTURE THOUGHTS

Once we apply truth to the stronghold, we know the enemy will bring other thoughts back at us:

"What makes you think you have value? Look at everything you have done. You are not the most intelligent person around. Nobody in his right mind would ever promote you."

We capture those thoughts by thinking about what we are thinking about. We grab them and hold onto them.

HAND IT TO JESUS

With our captured thoughts in hand, we give them to Jesus. This may be as simple as a prayer or as aggressive as writing our thoughts and putting them in the God box (see chapter 1).

FROM DISAPPOINTMENT TO HOPE

As I write this, our world is in crisis. COVID-19 (termed the "coronavirus") is wreaking havoc on the people of our planet. This pandemic is causing death and destruction. We are fearful, frustrated, and disappointed. Colleges are shut down. Public schools have closed for the remainder of the school year. Travel is all but dried up. Stores cannot keep supplies in stock. People are being laid off. Our state (like many others) just issued a "shelter-at-home" order. Church gatherings are solely online. Only essential businesses are open. Restaurants and bars are limited to takeout or delivery. Some countries and cities imposed a quarantine — people are only to leave their homes for dire emergencies.

As of now, we don't know when this pandemic will end. I do know that it is impacting every single person, denting our expectations. Since disappointment is caused by our expectations not being fulfilled, we are currently in a world-wide pit of disappointment.

We find a similar situation in the Old Testament book of Lamentations. A "lament" is defined as *"a passionate expression of grief or sorrow."*[17] Lamentations is full of laments: prayers and complaints to God from people who are walking in disappointment and grief. Here is a brief history:

Jeremiah (a prophet of God) witnessed the unravelling of the city of Jerusalem. Around 587 BC, the Chaldeans attacked Jerusalem. They burned down the king's palace and broke down the walls around the city. Those inside Jerusalem either fled or were carried off into exile (Jer 39:8-9). To say that the people of Israel were disappointed would be an understatement. In the middle of the chaos and grief, Jeremiah wrote the book of Lamentations. In doing so, he offers us several lessons, including how to move from disappointment to hope. Were Jeremiah alive today, he would tell us that the journey out of disappointment only happens by prayer. In Lamentations 1, Jeremiah offers three prayers, designed to move us from disappointment to hope.

THREE PRAYERS TO HELP US MOVE FROM DISAPPOINTMENT TO HOPE

Prayer #1: *God, look at my situation.*

"See, Lord, how distressed I am!
I am in torment within, and in
my heart I am disturbed, . . ."
(Lamentations 1:20; emphasis mine).

A disappointed Jeremiah prayed to God and asked the Lord to put eyes on the situation. Jeremiah knew that there is something powerful that happens when we invite someone into our disappointments.

The waitress probably thought that we were never going to leave. Sitting around a table were my buddies Jeremy, Brian, and I. While consuming eggs and some type of glorious cinnamon roll, we talked about life, family, and ministry. Brian and Jeremy are great friends. They serve in ministry and, well, not to sound cliché, but they "get me." They asked me how I was doing. I took a deep breath. "Well, guys, I am deeply disappointed, and I need some advice."

For the next hour I talked, and they listened. I shared with them a series of disappointments. I told them how each setback left me deflated and discouraged. My friends were gracious. They listened. They asked questions. They sympathized. I needed some advice from them, but I could not get advice without first inviting them to look at my situation.

I bet you have done something similar. I would venture that you have found yourself in a disappointing situation, and you reached out to someone for advice. Maybe you sought some advice from a pastor, teacher, friend, or counselor. But, before they offered you some advice, you first had to invite them to look at the situation.

It does not surprise me that we run to God with our disappointments. You know what continually surprises me? It surprises me that we run to Him *last*. Time after time we find ourselves running everywhere, and then (as if we just had the most brilliant idea in the world), we decide to take our disappointments to God. We ask Him to look at our situations. You would think He would be the first place we would run.

Writers of the Bible have penned several prayers, asking God to look at their situations. In Psalm 4, David writes,

> "Many are saying, 'Who will show
> us any good?' *Lift up* the light of *Your*
> *countenance* upon us, O Lord!"
> (Psalm 4:6; NASB, emphasis mine)

"Countenance" refers to a person's face or facial expression. David asks God to turn His face. A similar request is made in Psalm 80 where the author wrote "Restore us, Lord God Almighty; make your face shine on us, that we may be saved" (Psalm 80:19; emphasis mine).

In both instances, the request is the same: "God, turn Your face toward me." When God turns His face toward our situation, He takes in the whole picture, including our disappointment and grief. We invite Him into the mess. We give Him permission to walk around in the hurt and frustration. We bravely ask Him not only to help us but to search us (Psalm 139:24).

Maybe this is a good time to pause. If you are deep in disappointment, it's time for you to invite God in. Maybe you have been hesitant to do so because you feel like He has disappointed you. If that is the case, put it aside. He created you. He knows you. He loves you. He *likes* you. Give Him permission to take a deep inventory of your disappointment. What do you have to lose?

> He created you. He knows you. He loves you. He *likes* you.

When we ask God to turn His face to our disappointment, He sees the whole picture. He sees the good, the bad, the ugly, and the painful. Which brings us to our second prayer. In order to move from disappointment to hope, we not only pray, "God, look at my disappointment," we pray, "God, look at my pain."

Prayer #2: *God, look at my pain.*

In the middle of his disappointment, Jeremiah wrote:

> "See, Lord, how distressed I am!
> *I am in torment within, and*
> *in my heart I am disturbed*"
> (Lamentations 1:20; emphasis mine).

On the heels of asking God to look at his situation, Jeremiah gave a summary of the situation by saying, "I am in pain here!" I don't know how long it takes Jeremiah to admit that he is in pain, but I know that we often live in a place of denial.

"Nah, I'm good."

"It's nothing I can't handle."

"Other people have it worse than I do."

"I don't want to complain."

Maybe we would do well to say, "Look! I am in pain here."

When my brother Darel and I were younger, we loved fishing together. We spent most summers at the lake. Fishing was the chosen pastime. Our hope was to land a trophy fish (or any fish, really).

Late one afternoon Darel and I were standing on the shore. Best I can remember I was 11 years old; my brother was nine. I was casting; Darel was watching. We typically fished with an artificial lure, and that day was no different. This particular bait was equipped with six razor-sharp hooks designed to capture an aggressive fish. If everything went well, we would have

> If everything went well, we would have fresh fish for dinner.

fresh fish for dinner. "Let me do it," said Darel. I agreed, but before I did, I told him how it was going to work (I was, after all, the big brother). "I will cast it out," I said, "that way I can get the bait far out on the water, then you can reel it in." Darel agreed. Big mistake.

I stepped toward the shore with Darel behind me. Wanting to gain maximum distance in my cast, I whipped the pole and the lure over my shoulder. I immediately heard the lure hit something. "Woah," shouted Darel. Without turning around, I knew what had happened. I had snagged the trunk of a pine tree. This had happened a thousand times. I knew what to do. I needed to pull the bait off the trunk. Without turning around, I held the line tight and whipped the pole forward with great force. That's when I heard the scream.

> **That's when I heard the scream.**

I turned around. The lure had not hit a pine tree. It had hit the top of Darel's left hand. When it made contact, the razor-sharp hooks had snagged deep in his skin. When I yanked the bait (thinking I was freeing it from the trunk of the tree), I buried six razor sharp hooks deep in his hand.

I could count on one hand the number of times I have seen my father jog, let alone run. That day he became an Olympic sprinter. Running in the direction of the screams, he yelled, "What's wrong? What. Is. Wrong?" Darel was in too much pain to talk. Blood was dripping. He did the only thing he could do. He took his mangled hand

and lifted it towards our father as if to say, "Look! I am in pain."

Part of moving from disappointment to hope is telling God, "Look! I am in pain." Many of us don't want to acknowledge pain because we think it is no big deal. Wrong. It *is* a big deal. So big that you can't get out of it on your own. The irony is that our Father desires to help. He runs toward His kids when they cry out in pain.

Speak your pain to the Lord. Make a list. Bring Him up to date. Let Him know that your heart is crushed or that you are scarred. Invite Him in. Show Him your hand.

Let me wrap up the traumatic fishing story. My father grabbed a pair of needle-nose pliers and went to work like a skilled surgeon. He carefully removed the hooks from under the skin and tendons of Darel's hand. He washed my brother's mangled hand and wrapped it in a bandage for healing. Because of my father, Darel eventually made a full recovery. But our father would not have been able to heal if Darel had not shown him his hand.

Show the Father your pain. Right now. Take a few minutes. Get honest with God, He can handle your frustration. Invite Him to look into your situation. That may mean that you have to open up some old hurts from your past. It's alright. Our Father is a Healer, and He can handle the delicate surgery of fixing your heart. Show Him where you hurt. He will come running.

Show the Father your pain.

The third prayer of Jeremiah took a bit of a twist. Not only did he pray, "God, look at my situation," and "God, look at my pain," he offered a surprising appeal.

"God, look at my rebellion."

Prayer #3: *God, look at my rebellion.*

Sometimes our disappointment and grief can be traced back to hurts that are no fault of our own. However, sometimes our disappointments are direct results of stupid decisions that we have made. So many times, I have prayed, "God, why is this happening? This is not fair! I am in some pain here! Why, God? Why did You make this happen?" Once I get done whining, I sometimes hear the Lord say, "I didn't make this happen, you did. Your current disappointment is a direct result of sinful decisions that you have made. Stop blaming me for your rebellion." Ouch.

> **"Stop blaming me for your rebellion."**

Major respect to our friend Jeremiah. He realized that his disappointment was directly tied to his rebellion. Look at what he said:

> "See, Lord, how distressed I am! I am in torment within, and in my heart I am disturbed, *for I have been most rebellious*" (Lamentations 1:20; emphasis mine).

I was a good kid. I know most people say they were a good kid, but I really was. Really. I didn't give my parents grief. I stayed (mostly) out of trouble. I didn't backtalk, I ate my vegetables, did my chores and was not rebellious. My brother? Well, that's a different story. He liked to push the boundaries. Not me. I was the model child. Well... for the most part.

Because I was trustworthy, my parents rarely stayed up to make sure I got home by curfew. In high school, the drop-dead weekend curfew was midnight. If you hit the door at 12:01 AM, you had violated a most holy ordinance and would have to endure the wrath. However, because I was a golden child, my parents had no need to check on my arrival time. I was keenly aware of that fact.

One Friday night of my senior year, I broke curfew, not by a few minutes but by a few hours. I'll spare you the details of the said curfew-breaking activities but suffice to say that I was beyond late. However, since my parents trusted me, I knew they would not be waiting up. I would simply come home, quietly go to bed, and wake the next morning like nothing had happened. No harm, no foul.

The next morning, I ran into my then 16-year-old brother, Darel. Our conversation was brief. "I heard you come in at 3:00 a.m. You broke curfew, man." Whatever. This joker broke rules in his sleep. "Yea, well," I said, "just don't say anything."

Later that day I walked into the kitchen and ran smack into a heated debate between Darel and my mother. I don't remember what my brother was in trouble for (I lost count over the years). Evidently it had something to do with how he would not follow the rules (shocker). For some reason, my mom would not let it go.

She was digging hard into the insurgent. I didn't mind seeing the verbal correction. He deserved all this and more. I was rather enjoying watching the punishment. I contemplated making some popcorn, settling in, and watching my mother dispense justice on her rebellious son. That's when the situation went south. Recognizing my presence in the room, my mom turned. She pointed a finger at me. Looking back at my brother she said, "You! You should be more like your big brother. He never gives me any trouble. He obeys my rules. I don't ever have to worry about him. Why don't you try being more like your brother?"

Have you ever prayed for an escape hatch? Ever wished you could be secretly transported to another dimension? Ever prayed that Jesus would return at that

Have you ever prayed for an escape hatch?

exact moment? Yea, it was like that. Silence. I looked at my brother with eyes that said, "Don't. You. Dare." But he dared.

"Well," said my betrayer, "your perfect son broke curfew by three hours last night."

You know those moments in life where everything goes in slow motion? Where the fear seems all the greater and the wrath seems all the deeper? My mother slowly turned. I think I saw flames in her eyes and smoke in her ears. I don't remember exactly what she said, but her punishment was fast and swift. Grounded. An 18-year-old, near adult man, grounded. Wonderful.

For the next two weeks, I didn't go out. I was barely allowed to drive anywhere. I couldn't attend activities, and I couldn't have people over to the house. I was on lockdown. It was more than disappointing. As I took time to dissect the situation and find the reason I was in house-prison, I realized that the source of my grounding was not my mother. She was simply enforcing the rules. As much as I wanted to blame my brother, it was not his fault. The fault was my own. My rebellion had caused the punishment.

> **My rebellion had caused the punishment.**

Sometimes we are the source of our own disappointment. We sin. We step outside of the lines. We make poor decisions which result in disappointment and grief. Most of the time, we don't make these decisions knowing that they will result in disappointment. As a matter of fact, we don't even consider the future when we make these decisions. Jeremiah reminds us of this lack of judgement. He wrote that Israel's filthiness ". . . clung to her skirts; *she did not consider her future*" (Lamentations 1:9; emphasis mine).

He approached me and asked me for some spiritual guidance. He said that he was a follower of Jesus and was deeply in love with this girl. They were dating. Their relationship was going fabulously, and they would likely get married one day. They both knew that God brought them together. They loved serving Him, and they talked much about their walk with Christ. He asked what I thought about them moving in together before they got married. "Oh," I said, "that would be stupid." I went on to tell him that I could almost certainly predict his future. He would eventually drift away from the Lord. (It's hard to willfully continue to sin and maintain a vibrant relationship with Jesus.) It would start small. He and his lady would play house for a while, and then the fade would start. Less worship attendance, skip small group, pray later, get around to reading the Bible another day.

My advice-seeking friend didn't really want to hear what I had to say. He walked away and did what he had already decided to do. They moved in together. You know where they are now? Neither do I. But I know this: they drifted away from the Lord. My guess is that they are disappointed with the state of their spiritual lives, and they have one reason for their disappointment: They failed to consider their futures.

Our present actions will impact our future reality. The decisions we make now are not just for *now*. We must live wise, seek the Lord, and do what He says (James 1:22). Our rebellion has future consequences which often result in disappointment and grief.

What if we made poor decisions? What if our present life is a result of our rebellion? Good news. We have a God who picks us up, forgives us, dusts us off, and gives us a fresh start. This fresh start is summed up in my favorite verse:

If we confess our sins, he is faithful and just and will forgive us our sins and purify us from all unrighteousness. (1 John 1:9).

It is that simple. When we confess our rebellion, He forgives our sin. And when He forgives our sin, we move from disappointment to hope. We have hope of a better future in heaven, hope of a better future on earth, hope of a God who is with us, and much more. If your current disappointments are a result of your rebellion, confession is the key. Christ is waiting to forgive. Are you ready to ask?

A FINAL WORD AS WE MOVE FROM DISAPPOINTMENT TO HOPE

Life is not perfect. As such, it will be full of disappointments. Some of our disappointments are caused by our rebellion. In that case, we confess our rebellion and are forgiven. Some disappointments are caused because we live in a broken and busted world. The danger is that those disappointments want to chain us down. They want to drag our minds into a dark tunnel filled with lies:

"You will always be disappointed. You deserve to be disappointed. You are a disappointment. God wants you to wallow in grief."

Your enemy wants to use those lies to handcuff you. He sees you as a slave to your disappointment. Jesus, however, sees you differently. Listen to what the Apostle Paul writes:

"Therefore you are no longer a slave, but a son; and if a son, then an heir through God" (Galatians 4:7; emphasis mine).

Let that soak in. You are not a slave. You are a son. You are a daughter. And not just of anyone. You are a son or daughter of the Most High God. Your Father parts seas. Your Father forgives sins. Your Father raises the dead. Your Father erases the past. Your Father intersects your disappointments. Your Father offers hope.

May our disappointments (whether they have been done *by* us or *to* us) cause us to run to our Father. As we run, may we find the forgiveness that we need, a renewed mind and a transformed life.

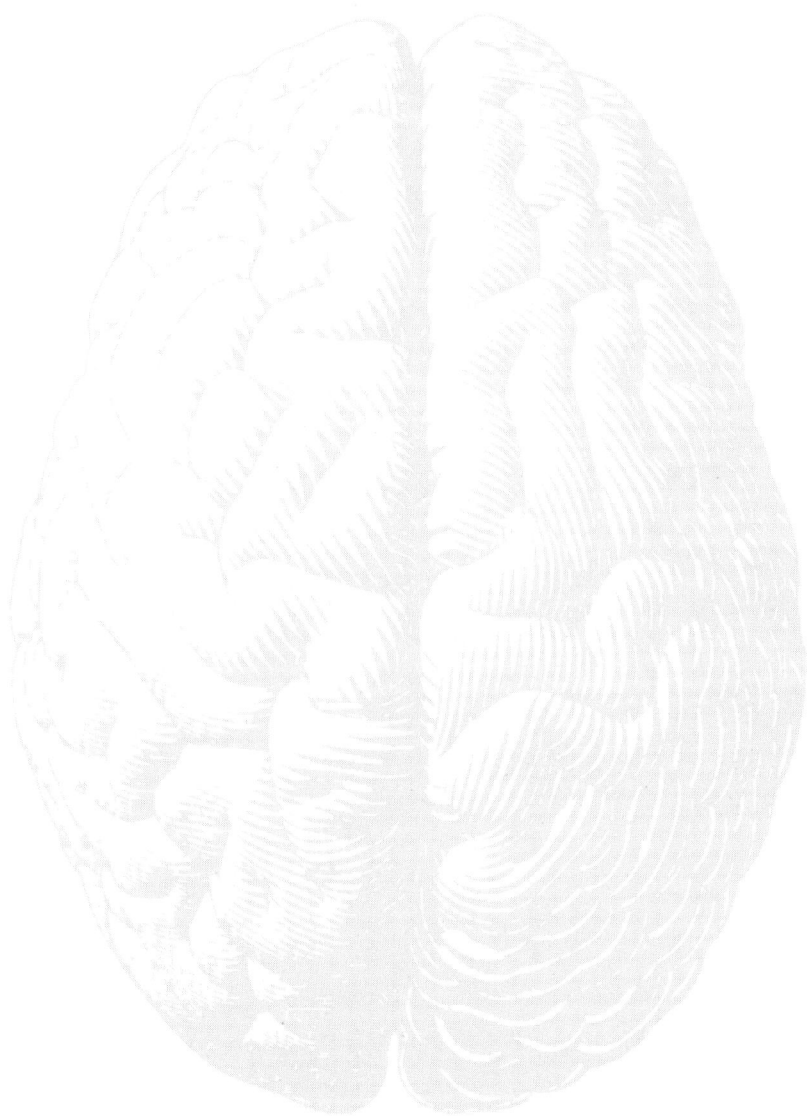

Final Words

In the end, we are left with a choice. Do we let our emotions rule us, or do we rule our emotions? In order for us to be transformed by the renewal of our minds (Rm 12:2), we must be proactive. This is not a one-and-done fight, but the more we learn how to fight, the easier it becomes. I promise.

The battle of emotions is a serious game. Sometimes an aggressive shift in our thinking will yield great results. Sometimes we have a chemical imbalance that needs identified. We may have a traumatic experience that needs explored. If you are wrestling with significant mental or emotional challenges, there is no shame in admitting that you need some help. I encourage you to reach out to a professional counselor. It may be that he can put you on a path to freedom as you take a deeper dive with someone who will partner with you.

For some, the mental battle may be incredibly difficult. You may have thoughts of self-harm or suicide. Perhaps you have even made an attempt to take your life. If you find yourself in a dark place, pick up your phone, and make a call to our friends at the Suicide Prevention Hotline, 1-800-273-8255.

You have all the tools you need in order to live a transformed life and ditch every negative emotion. Some days will be great, some will be hard; but know this: You are not alone. If you are a follower of Christ, you have a Father who is always present, and a Holy Spirit with power enough to raise the dead (Ephesians 1:18-20).

I believe in you. By reading this far in the book, you have proven that you have some fight in you. Congrats! When you feel yourself being pushed down, get back up. Dust yourself off. Lift your head. You are a child of the King. You are a friend of God. You are of great value.

Your future will not be defined by your past. Let the negative emotions come. You will DITCH them. You will go the extra mile and allow God to redeem your emotions. You will move toward a life greater than you dreamed.

My prayer for you is the same prayer that the Apostle Paul prayed:

"I pray that out of his glorious riches he may strengthen you with power through his Spirit in your inner being, so that Christ may dwell in your hearts through faith. And I pray that you, being rooted and established in love, may have power, together with all the Lord's holy people, to grasp how wide and long and high and deep is the love of Christ, and to know this love that surpasses knowledge—that you may be filled to the measure of all the fullness of God.

Now to him who is able to do immeasurably more than all we ask or imagine, according to his power that is at work within us, to him be glory in the church and in Christ Jesus throughout all generations, for ever and ever! Amen" (Ephesians 3:16-21).

Discussion Questions
Chapter 1: The *DITCH* Method

1. Describe a time that you tried to run away or "ditch" something. How did it turn out?

2. Have you ever run away from something only to find that it came around again? What was it?

3. In this chapter, you learn the *DITCH* Method. What does each letter stand for?

4. As you read chapter 1, what stood out to you?

5. Which of the *DITCH Method* steps is the easiest for you? Which is the most challenging?

Read 2 Corinthians 10:3–4.

6. One the keys of *DITCH*ing our emotions is identifying a stronghold. What is a stronghold?

7. What question do we need to ask in order to identify a stronghold?

8. Are there any strongholds that you have observed in other people's lives?

9. Are there any strongholds that you recognize in your own life?

Close with a time of prayer. Pray specifically for strongholds to be identified and for freedom to be found as we DITCH our emotions.

Discussion Questions
Chapter 2: From Anger to Justice

1. What is your favorite movie? Almost every movie is good vs. evil, so describe the fight between someone good and someone bad.

2. In your favorite movie, what was the motivation of the "good" character? Did anger play a part?

    Read Nehemiah 5:1-13. (Context: Jeremiah is leading a project of rebuilding the wall around Jerusalem. While doing so, he realizes that his fellow Jews have been taking advantage of each other, and he is angry.)

3. Why was Nehemiah angry?

4. What was the result of his anger?

5. In chapter two, you learned about using anger to fight injustice. What stood out to you?

6. Are there situations of injustice that are upsetting to you? What are they?

7. What would be the benefit of using anger to fight injustice?

8. How might the Lord want to use your anger to find injustice?

9. Are there any concrete steps that you could take to fight the injustice that makes you angry?

Close with a time of prayer. Pray for directed anger and the freeing of those who have been victims of injustice.

Discussion Questions
Chapter 3: From Annoyance to Protecting the House

1. What is your biggest pet peeve?

2. How do you react to your pet peeve?

3. In chapter three, you read about God using annoyance in order to make change. Did anything impact you as you read?

Read Nehemiah 13:1-9.

4. What stands out to you in the scripture above?

5. Are there any current situations that are annoying you?

6. What are some dangers of being annoyed but not taking action?

7. How might the Lord want to use annoyance to make a change?

8. What are some practical steps in order to move from annoyance to making a change?

9. Do you think Jesus is annoyed with our sin? What does He do about it?

    If Jesus turns His annoyance with our sin into action (He died on a cross, making it possible to erase our sin), it makes sense that He would ask us to use our annoyance to make a difference.

10. What is your next practical step out of annoyance?

Close with a time of prayer.

Discussion Questions
Chapter 4: From Sadness to Influence

1. If you had to guess who the saddest cartoon character of all time is, who would you guess?

2. More and more people seem to wrestle with sadness. Do you think this is because sadness is more prevalent or that more people are talking about sadness?

3. In chapter four you read about God turning your sadness to influence. What stood out to you as you read?

Read Nehemiah 2:1-12.

4. There are four steps from sadness to influence. Which of the steps is the easiest for you? Why?

5. Which of the steps is the hardest for you? Why?

6. Why do you think some people are stuck in sadness?

7. If someone feels stuck in sadness and asks you for help, what advice would you offer?

8. Part of moving out of sadness means we must face our fear and push through. Give an example of when you pushed through your fear.

9. Sometimes sadness comes from broken relationships. What does the Bible say our role is in mending broken relationships? (Romans 12:18)

10. If you are experiencing sadness, what is a practical next step you can take?

Close with a time of prayer. Pray that God will take us from sadness to influence.

Discussion Questions
Chapter 5: From Guilt to Deliverance

1. Describe a time as a kid when you did something and later felt a deep amount of guilt. What did you do with the guilt?

2. Do you think that most people feel guilty, or that most people don't let guilt bother them?

3. In chapter five, you learned about a vicious circle: sin - guilt - repentance - forgiveness peace and back again. Why do you think some people are stuck in the circle?

    Read Judges 3:12-23.

4. What jumps out at you in the scripture?

5. What do we learn about King Eglon in Judges 3:17?

6. There is danger in feeding our enemy and fattening him up. Why do you think that many of us keep feeding what is unhealthy in our lives?

7. Judges 3:18 suggests that Ehud walks out of the king's presence without killing him. In Judges 3:19, something changes Ehud's mind. What is it?

8. Think about the forces in your life that are causing guilt. In order to go from guilt to deliverance, something must die. In your life, what must die? How will you kill it?

9. Describe what your life would look like if you were delivered from guilt. How would it change your attitude and your outlook on life?

Close with prayer.

Discussion Questions
Chapter 6: From Fear to Identity

1. In the early 2000s, NBC produced a show called *Fear Factor*. Participants were challenged with tasks such as eating slimy bugs, being buried alive, or lying down and letting rats run over them (as well as a hundred other fear-filled scenarios). If you were a contestant on *Fear Factor*, what challenge would make you walk away without even making an attempt at winning?

2. In chapter six, you explored fear and anxiety. What impacted you in this chapter?

   Read Luke 12:4-7.

3. What do you think Jesus is trying to say when He talks about the value of sparrows?

4. Do you think most people feel valuable? Why or why not?

5. Think about the most valuable item you have ever seen. What is it? What is it worth? Who determines the value?

6. Someone once said, "An item is only worth what someone is willing to pay for it." If you were kidnapped and kept for ransom, how much would someone be willing to pay for you?

7. If you were kidnapped and kept for ransom, how much would Jesus pay for you?

Read Mark 10:45.

8. How much did Jesus pay for you?

9. If an item is only worth what someone is willing to pay for it, Jesus must see tremendous value in you. Discuss.

Close with prayer.

Discussion Questions
Chapter 7: From Discouragement to Courage to Freedom

1. Of all the superheroes, who has the most courage? How does he or she show courage?

2. In the *Wizard of Oz*, who was the character with the least amount of courage? How did he act?

3. In Chapter seven, you discovered how to move out of discouragement and into courage. As a result, you find freedom. What impacted you in this chapter?

   Read Judges 4:4–14.

4. What stands out to you?

   Read Judges 4:14.

   One of the steps out of discouragement is that we look for God's movement.

5. Where have you seen God move in the past?

6. Where do you see Him moving right now in the lives of people in your group?

7. Where do you see Him moving right now in your life?

His movement in our lives produces courage and eventually freedom. Close with prayer. Ask that this week you can see His movement and find the courage that we need.

Discussion Questions
Chapter 8: From Apathy to Identity

1. Have you ever dressed up in a costume (maybe for a party or Halloween)? What was your favorite costume?

2. If you could be anyone for 24 hours, who would it be? Why?

3. Do you think most people are satisfied with who they are? Why or why not?

4. In chapter eight, you explored moving from apathy to identity. As you read the chapter, what impacted you?

Read Psalm 100:3.

Read Romans 14:8.

5. What do these verses have in common?

6. If you are a parent, how would you describe your child to someone?

7. How do you think God would describe you? This is a deep question. You may want to take some time and write down your answer - just between you and the Lord.

Select one person from your group. Have your group answer this question: «What would Jesus say about this person?" Once a few have shared, move to the next person.

Close with prayer.

Discussion Questions
Chapter 9: From Disappointment to Hope

1. Describe the most disappointing car you have ever owned OR describe the most disappointing class you have ever taken.

2. Name one disappointment you have experienced in the last three weeks.

3. In chapter nine, you explored the journey from disappointment to hope. Did anything stand out to you?

Read Lamentations 1:20.

4. One of the prayers in Lamentations 1:20 is the prayer "God, look at my pain." Why would the writer pray such a thing?

5. What do you think God would say about the pain or disappointment that you may be experiencing?

6. What is the benefit of telling God your frustrations?

7. What do you think the Lord wants to do with your frustrations?

8. Give an example from your life where your frustrations led you to some sort of hope.

9. We find a great amount of hope (and less disappointment) when we remember who we are.

   Read Galatians 4:7.

10. Who does it say we are?

Close by sharing and praying over any current disappointments.

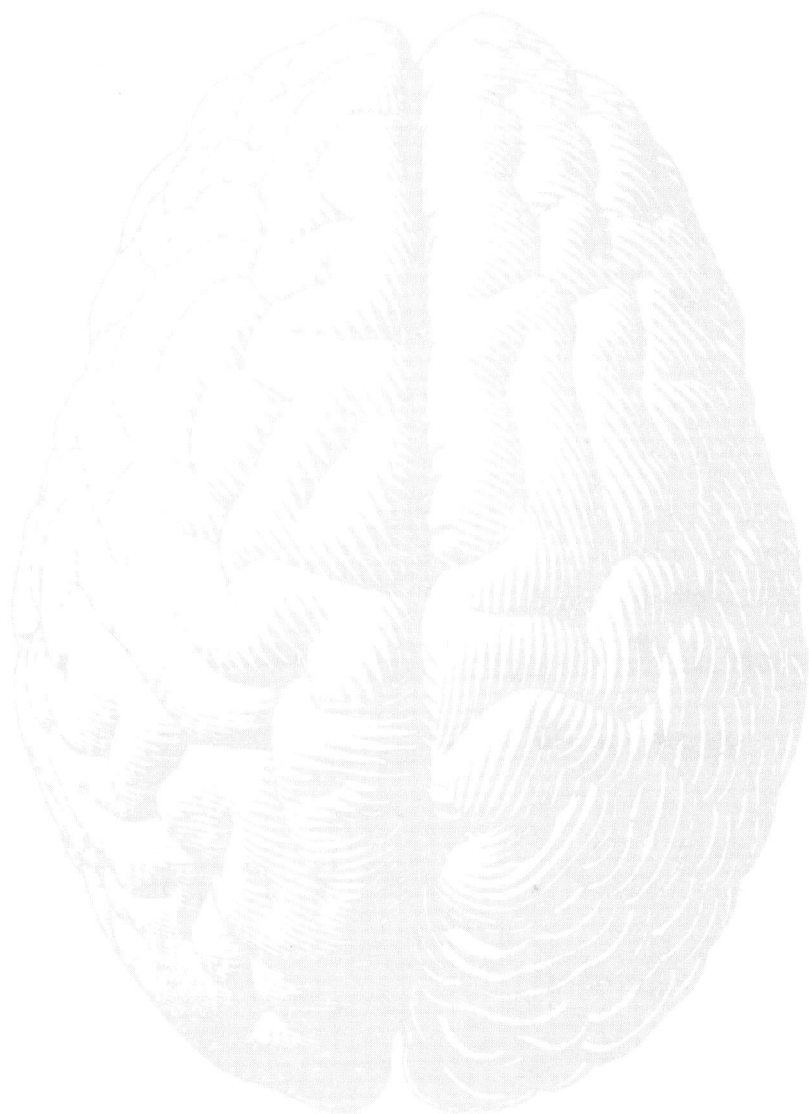

Sources

1. Kelly, Megan (2015, June). *How Prayer Changes the Brain and the Body.* www.renewingallthings.com/how-prayer-changes-the-brain-and-body/
2. www.biblehub.com/greek/3794.htm
3. www.merriam-webster.com/dictionary/pretension
4. Groeschel, Craig. *Mastermind.* www.life.church/media/mastermind/the-peace-of-god/
5. www.azquotes.com/quote/494880
6. www.azquotes.com/quote/763669
7. www.lexico.com/en/definition/purge
8. www.biblestudytools.com/dictionary/baptize-baptism
9. www.georgeaddair.com
10. Eastman, Dick. *The Hour that Changes the World* (Baker Publishing, 2002) 33-34
11. Johnson, John (2019, December) *How Much Hair Loss in Normal?* www.medicalnewstoday.com/articles/327188
12. Cushatt, Michele. *Relentless. The Unshakable Presence of a God who Never Leaves.* (Zondervan Publishing, 2019) 62
13. www.merriam-webster.com/dictionary/liquidate

14. Seltzer, Leon. (2016, April) *The Curse of Apathy: Sources and Solutions*. www.psychologytoday.com/us/blog/evolution-the-self/201604/the-curse-apathy-sources-and-solutions

15. www.nationalgeographic.org/encyclopedia/equator/

16. www.merriam-webster.com/dictionary/disappointment

17. www.merriam-webster.com/dictionary/lament

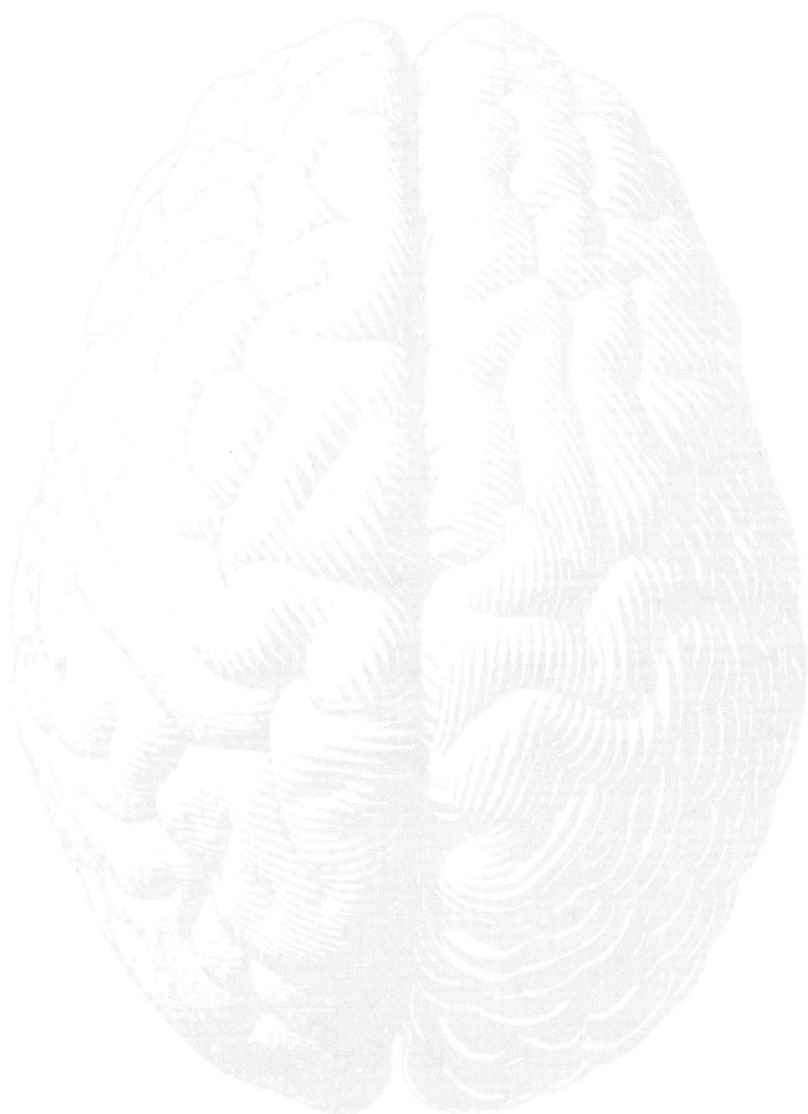

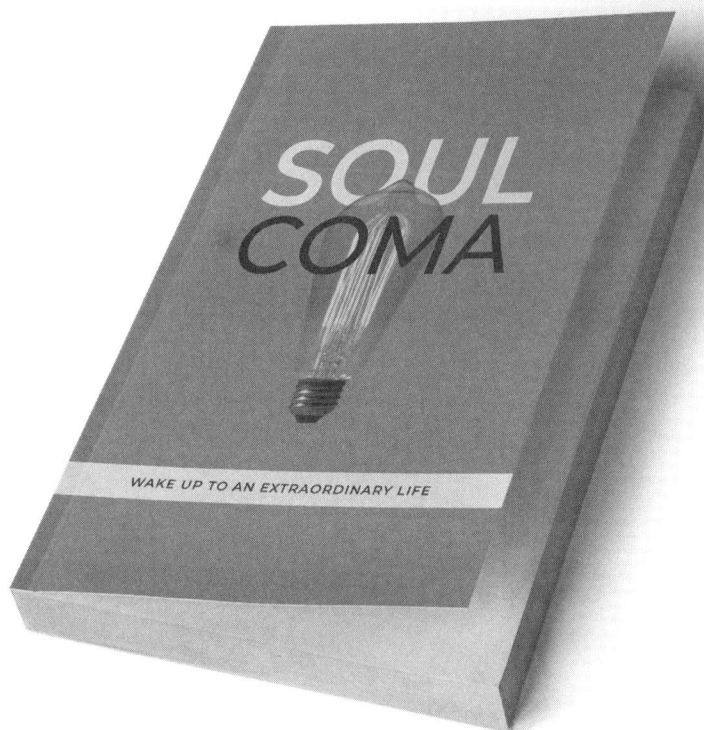

WAKE UP TO AN EXTRAORDINARY LIFE

RESUSCITATE
YOUR SPIRITUAL LIFE

In Soul Coma: Wake up to an Extraordinary Life,
Pastor Scot Longyear explores seven practices to awaken
your relationship with Christ.

Using sound biblical principles, real-life stories, and abundant
humor, Scot will help inspire and equip you to live the vibrant
spiritual life you have always imagined.

Available at ScotLongyear.com

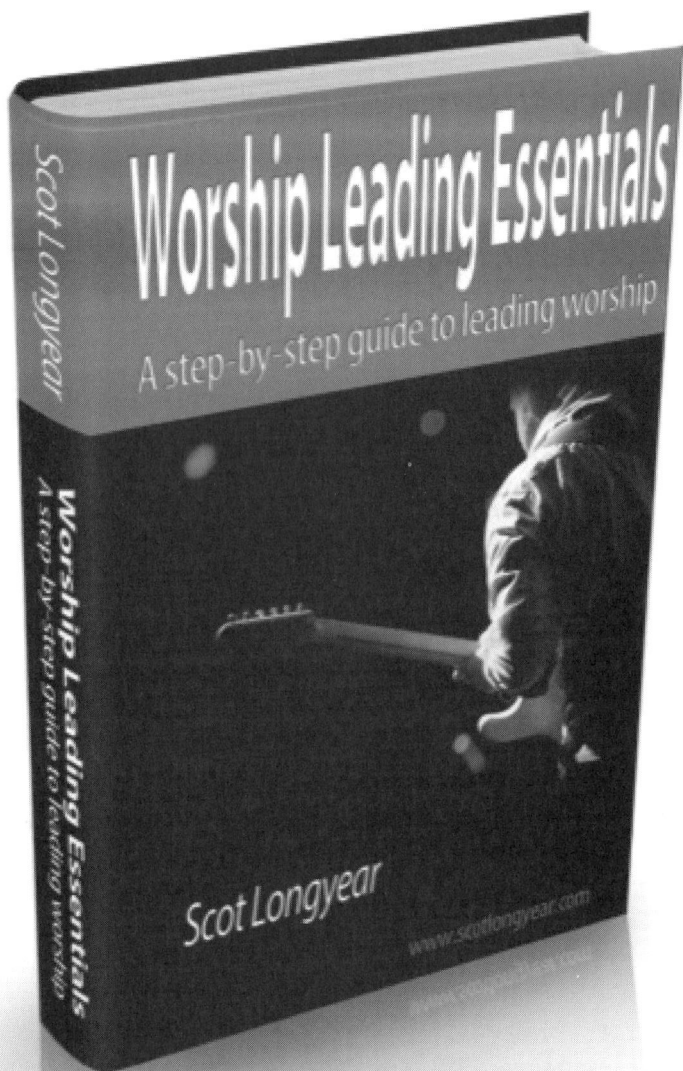

Worship Leading Essentials

A step-by-step guide to leading worship

Scot Longyear

www.scotlongyear.com

Worship Leading Essentials

Worship Leading Essentials is a 70-page ebook designed to help worship leaders lead with greater impact. This step-by-step guide is a collection of lessons Scot has learned while leading worship for more than 20 years.

Worship Leading Essentials addresses such topics as . . .

- Personal spirituality
- How to deal with band conflict
- How to put together a set list
- How to leverage criticism
- Much more

Some have used *Worship Leading Essentials* as a study guide for their worship teams, reading a chapter and discussing each week before rehearsal.

Whatever your level of worship leading, *Worship Leading Essentials* is a step-by-step guide to making you and your team more effective worship leaders.

To download *Worship Leading Essentials*, visit scotlongyear.com.

For more info, check out
www.scotlongyear.com